Free Bird

Free Bird

Copyright © 2025 by **Booklyn Writers**

All rights reserved. No part of this book may be reproduced, distributed, or transmitted in any form or by any means, including photocopying, recording, or other electronic or mechanical methods, without the prior written permission of the publisher.

Edition: First

ISBN: 979-8-89397-842-1

Published by **Booklyn Writers**

As you see it, so shall you be it

Table of Contents

Preface 5

In the Beginning 7

A new direction 16

Everything is in place 23

Echoes of the past remain 32

New Year's Resurrection 41

The end of the road 51

Time to say hello and goodbye 63

Finding my way 77

Fate Finds it's Mark 87

Mirrors of authenticity 104

Welcome Home 120

Preface

Light has a way of showing up in the most unlikely places. This account of a life lived, is an extreme example of the human condition and the effects of innocents trampled by fearful hearts. My intention is to allow my journey to be laid wide open in hopes you can relate and see that we are all made of the same fabric and suffer the same fate to a greater or lesser degree. Freedom from the human condition is possible and you will see clearly how it came to me. This is not a book to follow as a blueprint to your process. It's just a very detailed account of my transition from fear to freedom. It's not a study guide or new philosophy. What it is, is real and heartfelt struggles and triumphs. It's a person that felt unworthy in every way and was given a miracle that changed everything. Light in the midst of darkness. The changes that lie ahead for humanity surely require compassion and understanding. An open mind and a willing heart will navigate the coming change with grace...

Free Bird

Free Bird

In the Beginning

Well into the night my heart pounded in fear. I wondered what is happening to me. I continued to spiral while the lady downstairs taps on the ceiling in protest to my pacing. My mind is racing with thoughts of, What do I do? I don't know. Something is wrong, really wrong, it's some kind of brain damage or something, I know it. Wait, the girl next door is dating a doctor. God please let him be there. Frantically I knocked on the door. Looking interrupted she calls him over. I explain my dire situation as he listens with concern at first. Then concern turns to loss of interest as he checks me out. He suggested that I go to the emergency room, if I felt it necessary.

Returning to my apartment with one foot in the grave, I felt alone in my conviction. With no help on the horizon my fear intensified. I continued my pacing with all thoughts holding up my hopeless situation. Full-on panic set in, with a stark reality that I'm not going to make it. In total horror of impending death, I turned to start another pacing circuit and like a light switch, complete silence. Like a stopper being pulled, I felt all the pressure and thoughts drain from my head. A feeling of peace and complete relief washed over me, with a strange sensation of my location moving from my head to my chest.

Overcome with a feeling completely foreign to me, I struggled to make sense of it. I feel light as a feather and empty of all concerns that just a moment ago carried a death sentence. Calling on a lifetime of varying degrees of anxiety and depression, I had nothing to compare this feeling to. Convinced that somehow I just escaped death, I wanted to share my good fortune. I called my parents at a late hour, waking them up. I have never spoken so freely with them. A total lack of fear became evident as I spoke with conviction and even love. Speaking like this was foreign to my family. Two hours went by in a flash. The words I love you crossed my lips for the first time in memory, as I hung up. At thirty-three years old my whole world opened up to possibilities previously thought out of reach. Morning found me still inspired and full of energy. Thoughts began to reestablish their presence in the empty space that appeared the night before. Although they had a more positive energy of what the future holds. From that day forward, my life took on a new direction.

Over the next couple of weeks, the familiar thoughts of worry and not being good enough filtered back in. That fueled a very determined search to regain the experience of that fateful night on January 4th 1998. I attributed the escalating fear of that night to be a mix of a fever combined with antibiotics and cold medicine. It would be years before I would better understand the release from the intense fear that followed. For those couple short weeks, I stretched out and gained confidence that I desperately sought after to that point in my life. Everything improved, my work, hobbies and most importantly, to feel and speak freely to everyone around me.

Free Bird

Up until this happened there was really only one lasting interest in my life. I had a real love for my work and it was the only place I found a sense of belonging. I came to it many years prior in the fall of 1984. Nineteen and clueless to what I was going to do for a living, I found work with a small roofing company. On this one particular job they needed to hire a crane company to enable us to deliver the stone from the trucks to the newly installed rubber roof. A sizable job for us that also held prominence in the community. It was one of two glass factories in town that was a major source of employment. My job was to open the shoot on the truck and fill the hopper, then the crane would lift the hopper to the roof where it was distributed over the rubber as a protective layer. I would have breaks between trucks and would take that opportunity to speak to the crane operator. He was only too happy to share his stories of operating all kinds of different equipment and work that he had done. He had me hanging on every word as if a new world was being revealed to me. In those short few days a fire was started in my heart that burned fiercely throughout my entire career.

I started to build momentum in a short time and enrolled in a two-year course for service and operation of heavy equipment at Williamsport Area Community College. In less than a year from listening to the inspiring stories that found my heart, I was hands on learning the trade. For the first time in my life I was all in and gave it everything I had. I studied hard with even things I didn't like, feeling that it was all a reflection of my dream. No doubt my love for this vocation was real and carried me along with a feeling that I will do whatever it takes to succeed. It didn't however relieve me of what by now was my normal state of social awkwardness and feeling that I'm not right somehow. I did very well in college and graduated with a respectable GPA and respect from my teachers. As for my social success in what appeared to be filled with great opportunities. It was just business as usual feeling awkward and ill prepared for any meaningful connection. My past relationship experience was just a mix of possibilities which quickly ended due to my discomfort with emotional connection. Likely due to the discomfort that I felt about myself. I did develop strong feelings for one girl that ended in heartbreak and set me back for many years to come. It was a difficult and strange situation wanting something that I was afraid of.

After college I was offered a job near Reading Pennsylvania for a small contractor. Work like I wanted was scarce in my little town in northwestern PA. I packed my car and moved four hours away. I was excited for the work but sad to leave the comfort and support of home. Living for months in a motel I was finally able to find an apartment north of Reading. My skills developed quickly and soon bigger doors opened and I joined the local union where the sky was the limit. I was fortunate to land a job with a contractor that I could grow with and learn my trade. After a year or so I moved to the Harrisburg area where most of their work was. Things started to open up for me socially as I shared an apartment with a buddy from college. Slowly I started to develop a social network of acquaintances and friends at work and my increasing interest in playing pool. One friendship in particular was dear to me. An older gentleman who was referred to as "Big Daddy." He is a very charismatic type with a kind demeanor that had a way of making me feel good and was a real blessing to my lack of social skills. We met at work and he was also an operator. He kind of took me under his wing and shared little tricks of the trade. I was very lucky to have skilled operators all around me willing to help me along.

We often met on Thursday night at a local bar and restaurant. He had a welcoming way about him that people flocked to. Always engaged in conversation he helped me come out of my shell a bit and made me feel like I was a part of something. Soon he was inviting me up to his camp on weekends and my social circle continued to expand. One weekend at camp we went to breakfast and I took a liking to one of the waitresses. I could not bring myself to talk with her and Big Daddy wouldn't have it and said to her, " we are not leaving until you give him your number." Sure enough, her number was written on the check when she laid it on the table. It lasted a couple months and was a welcome change after years of very little. It happened that her ex-boyfriend started showing more interest in her and feeling a possible rejection, I ended it. Although socially more opportunities were opening, I was still dysfunctional as ever.

I continued to excel at work and decided to change directions with a new opportunity. A large three-year road job kicked off nearby and I somehow landed in a key position at the young age of twenty-seven. It was just another great adventure in a job I loved. A whole new set of friendships started to take shape. One in particular was a quick-witted mechanic named Tyson. He was well experienced and good at his job, always with the humor he was a joy to be around. We worked very long hours and there was very little social activity outside work. One day in conversation he mentioned that the girl he was seeing had a daughter around my age that was single. Of course I was all ears as he explained, Sandy also works as an operator newly hired on a job he helped her get. He made sure that she was at the next union meeting and we met and made plans for a date. After a couple of dates, I felt it wasn't going to go anywhere. I had a kind of all or nothing mentality and steered clear of casual dating for the most part. The sting of hurting someone kept me isolated even more. At the same time loneliness would get the better of me and I would give myself permission to engage further. Thinking why not maybe this can be just a casual thing and the next date she spent the night. I remember Tyson poking at me a bit in fun on Monday morning. Often working twelve and fourteen hours a day, the next evening I'm working near an exit ramp. I noticed Tyson's mechanic truck rolling past me and his girlfriend was with him. Being maybe fifty feet away as they passed, she glanced at me with a piercing look in her eye. There was a heaviness to it that I had not seen before. My phone rang eleven thirty that night. It was Sandy's mom. In a broken and shaking voice she said there was an accident at work and Sandy was killed.

I was caught in the most awkward conversation of my life. Tragically she was thrown from the machine and it rolled over her. I was unable to show appropriate feelings and went into protection mode and said things like, if there is anything I can do. I lay there in shock trying to wrap my head around it, even worse she had a five-year-old son. Certainly I was sad and felt compassion for the situation but that quickly was overshadowed by, my God, how am I going to get through this. Clueless on proper propensity for such a difficult and tragic event I stopped to visit. Tyson met me outside. He was completely drained of any hint of his wit or humor. My situation grew even more awkward as I realized they looked at me as a significant part of Sandy's life. I left there feeling a total imposter that had no right to any goodwill. My mind raced to figure out how to get through this. The funeral was set and I sent a modest flower arrangement feeling that I was a very small part of her life.

The day of the funeral I walked into the church to see my flowers prominently displayed in the center. Could it get any worse I thought and sat in the back out of sight. No way could I face them feeling so unworthy of their attention. Sounds of sorrow rang out as the music played and the minister spoke. At the end I slipped out the back still unseen. From there I drove to the cemetery and waited until most people were seated under the tent at the grave site. Then I snuck in and sat in the back again. The family is sitting in front of the casket ready to be lowered in, covered in flowers. The minister said a few things then all attention was on Sandy's best friend as she gave the eulogy. It was the most heartfelt and touching thing that I had ever heard. With such honesty and openness, I had the privilege to get to know Sandy from her friend's heart. She carried on with tears rolling down her face and I sat in awe of her fearless conviction. I loved every bit of it as her inspiring words touched everyone's heart. When she finished, she picked up a tray of short stemmed red roses and starting with Sandy's son she handed them out to the closest people in Sandy's life. Gracefully she pins each rose on with love, and then with the last rose in hand she heads straight for me. Mortified and exposed, I became the center of attention. Gently she pins that last rose on my jacket as our eyes met for the first time. It was too much and without hesitation I quickly walked off in tears. Inconsolable as I head to my car, I hear someone call my name. It's our local business agent and he insists that I talk with him. Still unable to pull myself together, he says that every day it will get better and better and I will be okay.

I am not sure how long it took me to figure out why I reacted so strongly that day to a rose given by what seemed to be love itself. The insight that I gained from that experience became a central understanding of my dysfunction. Having deprived myself of any real consideration, feeling unworthy and certain of not being good enough. I was faced with something too contrary to my own belief. The tears of that day were from a soul so deprived of love that to be included in such a sacred and loving way was maybe the first time in my life I felt truly accepted and connected to something so lovely.

My relationship with Tyson became more distant after that and I was now even more reluctant to pursue a relationship. My work continued to rule my life and called for me to move once again. I moved to Scranton PA, for continued employment with the same company. It was here that my life found a new direction. Still my heart longed for love but it seemed impossible. My whole life consisted of longing for something I didn't feel worthy of. The only bright spot in my life was my work. Somehow, the accolades of doing something I loved gave me a feeling of self worth that exceeded the norm. Through my driven passion I was able to elevate my perceived standing by identifying with above-average abilities. This didn't however carry over into my social life.

Until the events of that night in a third-floor apartment in Scranton, all I knew in life was struggle with a slight relief through identifying with my accomplishments. All my focus in life was given to the idea that if I can become good enough and build myself up, I will gain recognition and feel worthy. Finally, I will rid myself of this god-awful feeling that I am not right. With the lessening of this feeling that came with accomplishment, this seemed to me the only way to gain freedom from the tyranny of my own mind. Triumph through accomplishment solidified itself as my only way out. Then that night happened and turned my whole world upside down. Peace beyond anything I could have imagined came to me in the midst of hell. Contrary to everything my world was built on. How could this be? A new love came into my heart that night and it never let go.

A new direction

Very much like the drive I developed at the start of my career, I was all in to find a way back to the experience of that night. I moved to Allentown in the spring of 1998 for work on another big project. This move really held promise for me. My career was taking off as my reputation spread. I was on a mission and everything I needed was in the Lehigh Valley. Open to any and all ways to help improve myself I started with therapy. I remember my first session brought some reflection on my need to be special. I said to her with subtle desperation that I was going to be an interesting and uncommon client. She immediately fired back and said that all of her clients were interesting and special in their own way. It might have been the first time that a light was shone on this ever-present need that plagued me.

With no clue on how to reclaim this mysterious state of peace, I turned to the local Barnes & Noble. The self-help section became my favorite go-to. Almost every weekend I would browse looking for answers to my problems. I would walk out of there, book in hand and a feeling that this is it. Over the course of a few days to a couple of months I would gain insights and a feeling of progress and when the progress reverted back to the old, I would move on to the next book. Before I knew it, I had filled an entire bin with self-help books. My therapist suggested a meeting called Co-Dependence Anonymous. She said it was helpful to some of her patients to gain social skills and develop healthy relationships. It proved to be a great source of understanding as well as social opportunities for me. It was here that I came to know something that began to lighten my load. Between the self-help books and the new perspective in therapy and Coda, I began to realize that I was not alone. Up until this time I felt I was the only one that had this problem. Sure, there were people with issues but I always reserved myself to be alone in my feeling of not being right.

One day, I'm in Barnes & Noble. I held two books in my hand and could not decide. The one had an interesting review displayed on the back. It was by an already famous author and I thought this was a real testament to its legitimacy. The book was The Power of Now by Eckhart Tolle. I bought it as an audiobook so I could listen to it in my car and even at work. I was blown away by it and knew that this was what I was looking for. His account of an experience that turned his whole life around was very similar to mine. From that point on, for many years, he was the only author I paid any attention to. Eckart's teaching opened up a whole new world for me. Though not contrary to other perspectives his clarity and light-handed insights gave a sense of real wisdom. I listened over and over and slowly I came to know that what he said was for real. I continued to go to the meetings and therapy. Socially things started to improve with new friends from the meeting and work.

Although my ultimate goal was a return to a permanent state of peace. I was unable to let go of the idea that achievement along with a loving relationship was the way to get there. If there was anything that held the promise to deliver, I tried it. With little success in finding love I thought maybe geography would bring new possibilities. A whole other country on the other side of the world should do it. After much research I found the perfect place. The people have been voted to be some of the nicest in the world. With its breathtaking beauty and great reviews from people I talked to, I booked a month-long trip to New Zealand. Surely this would bring opportunities that I did not have here in the States. I imagined people that would be so nice I would feel welcomed and at ease. It was a wonderful trip filled with great adventure and thrilling experience but my discomfort around people was just the same and so were the results.

Undeterred, I quickly set my sights on my next idea. If I wasn't able to gather enough confidence to approach women then I will make myself more appealing and draw them in. My work was going well and I was able to save a good amount of money. As soon as I got back from New Zealand I started shopping for a sports car. Never one to take half measures, I ordered a brand-new Corvette. This would most certainly increase my chances for love. Even more than that it would increase my stature in every part of my life. What an exciting time for me. Work was at an all-time high with people taking note of my skills, new friends and now the car on its way. I could barely contain my excitement picking up the car. I felt myself increase in importance and value. Watching for people to notice me driving it, showing up at the Coda meetings with it, I felt ten feet tall. Finally, I found something that gave me a sense of importance other than work.

Free Bird

Piece by piece I was constructing an undeniable master piece that would once and for all remove my feelings of not being good enough. In my mind only one thing remained to complete my portrait. The love of a beautiful wife. This would put to rest any doubts anyone had that I wasn't normal and maybe even above average. Amazingly a beautiful girl was hired at my work and assigned to my crew. Outgoing and hard working I thought this could be it. We flirted back and forth as we got to know each other. Others even mentioned that we were perfect for each other. My fear overran my ability to advance on her and we drifted apart. What a strange dilemma I was in, too picky to settle for average and too afraid to approach a beautiful woman.

My one quality that carried me is, I would stop at nothing to get what I wanted. As I got more comfortable at the Coda meetings, romantic possibilities started there also. Eventually one came into focus and before I knew it, I was in a relationship. Maybe not the best place to find someone, a meeting for people that are dysfunctional in relationships. So attractive though someone that knows all the rules of dysfunction. Within two months I knew I had to get out and three months later my backbone grew strong enough to do it. Train wreck or not, I was making progress and was determined as ever. Breaking down my issue of fear and how it stopped me from the ability to approach women, I started to consider psych drugs as a possible answer. Talking with my therapist she recommended a doctor within her workplace. He described how my brain wasn't making enough of certain chemicals and these drugs would bring balance and relief. It took some time to find the right drug and dose but in a short few months I started to notice real change. Every part of my life started to improve. I started to feel more relaxed and more open to people. After all my searching to fix myself, just as I thought, there was something wrong and now it's been fixed. The future hadn't looked this bright since I began my intense search for peace.

After eight years of working for a road contractor, I felt it was time for change. Work was booming in the Lehigh Valley and it was an easy transition back to where my career started in building work. Laying down my lofty status after years of development, I was ready for a new challenge. Armed with my newfound confidence I quickly rose through the ranks. I would often gain friends through respect, regarding my ability and this new job soon yielded one who had similar interests and relationship status. One weekend he recommended that we go to this place called the Shanty. He said the crowd was a nice mix and they offered live music. We met at a sports bar first and killed some time till things warmed up at the Shanty. Arriving, I immediately liked the vibe. The Shanty was upscale with a nice dining area and a separate bar where the band was playing. It was a cover band that had a local following named Jake Kaligis. A passionate artist that played a great mix of hits.

Already there was a nice crowd gathered with a full bar. Immediately I start to scan for potential women. I noticed one across the bar by herself. She was attractive with a very noticeable confidence that seemed out of place. She moved about as if she owned the place, talking with the band and the bartenders.

Fascinated, I watched her display qualities that I only dreamed of. I was feeling more confident but certainly not enough to approach this woman. There was another that I had been keeping my eye on. Her back was to me and I hadn't gotten a good look at her. Then like a gift from heaven she turned to her right and I was blown away. The profile of her face is still fresh in my memory. Long dark hair with matching eyes. I looked on her as if she held the key to everything. I walked to the bar beside her and ordered a drink. I said hello and was greeted with an open and inviting reply. Very much like my confusion about the woman with misplaced confidence, she had a welcoming way about her that was uncommon for a beautiful woman.

We stayed in conversation to my delight and eventually invited my friend to join us. He engaged with her friend and we continued in light conversation. At one point Katie, the angel that I was speaking to, got up to go to the bathroom. And like my buddy said, she's tall. Five inches taller without the three-inch heels she was wearing. I was a bit confused. She is tall and beautiful and I am short and didn't think I was good looking. She was certainly unlike anyone I have met before. I figured she knew my stature while she talked to me so I am just going to go with it. We stayed till closing and the lights came on and so did the advances on her. Two separate men approached her with interest as if I wasn't even there. Like a Hail Mary, one even left his card. Unfazed, she continued to have interest in me and we decided to go to a local diner for breakfast. There she surprised me with interest in what I was doing tomorrow. I said a pool tournament and in my further disbelief she implied that she would like to go. Of course yes, and I picked her up at ten a.m., only a few hours after saying goodnight. I walked into that pool room like I was the man, with all eyes on her. I didn't win the tournament but I walked out of there feeling I won something far more valuable.

She invited me into her home where I was met with an over-the-top greeting by her golden retriever Sweety. A dog lover myself, the good vibes continued to increase. We sat on her couch and talked some more and in another unbelievable gesture she gently laid her head on my lap. Stunned in processing the events that I have been blessed with in less than twenty-four hours. I sit with an angel under my left hand and a loving dog named Sweety under my right. Goodbye for now, as her ex was due to drop off her two kids Kyle and Denise. I had already made peace with the idea that kids may be a part of finding love, as I was already thirty-seven years old. The height difference though, was something that I hadn't considered and if not for her being seated when I first saw her, we likely would never have met. March 2nd, 2002, would turn out to be another turning point in my life, the day love came knocking.

Everything is in place

Her gentle kindness combined with her stunning looks gave me a sense of mystery. She possessed this very natural accepting way that was almost completely free of criticism or judgment. Till now my closest experience to this was a grandmother's love. The mystery of the overly confident woman the night we met was revealed in grand fashion. She turned out to be part of the band and brought the house down with her amazing vocals.

There was a hurdle that I would have to overcome. It wasn't the height difference that I might have thought. It was her open acceptance of me. She had the looks to elevate my worth in appearance. Yet at the same time gave me a sense of actual worth reflected in her eyes. Strange as it may seem I was more comfortable with someone that held up the low opinion I had of myself. Oh I tried to make the height thing a deal breaker but she wouldn't flinch or give me reason to fear rejection. Almost against my nature we proceeded to build trust and direction. Only two weeks in she invited me to stay and meet the kids after being dropped off. At ages nine for Denise and ten for Kyle they were already developed with unique personalities. Feeling more confident that she had real potential I picked her up for a date in the vette. She took it in stride and barely made mention of it. Later revealing that she was impressed but with her I knew it wouldn't have made a difference if I only had my old Chevy truck.

Seeing real possibilities, I committed to no overnights until I was reasonably sure this was for real. Slowly, I opened myself up to three new people and an awesome dog. Before I knew it my life was full of concerts and movies and even a family vacation to Virginia Beach. Not once did she waiver, like she instinctively knew I was a flight risk. And after six months it was decided that I would move in. Our relationship was unlike anything that I have known or even witnessed. There was no euphoria stage, we were the same in the beginning as any other time in our relationship. More than that we were the same in public as we were at home. We had nothing to hide or nothing to inflate for display. I am sure I gave her plenty of reason to curse me over the years but the most I can remember is one well deserved jerk as she walked away.

Not above the occasional romantic gesture or surprise, I saved all the stubs from our first year and framed them. On our first-year anniversary we returned to the Shanty even wearing the same clothes for effect. The framed event display was a homerun and a solid witness to something I thought may never happen. Disciplined in my approach I wasn't going to take a single step that didn't have a firm foundation. As our relationship gave me security in its direction, I lost interest in therapy and Coda meetings, yet lasting friendships endured. Eckhart, still alive in my heart, continued to pave the way and became my only source of spiritual knowledge. My skills at work continued to escalate and soon my reputation was similar to that of my road work accomplishments. Everything was working for me. In a short five years since my life-changing event, my life was filled with good things. Most precious of which lay beside me night after night in complete comfort. I remember many a night, I would wake and lay there in gratitude. I also had a strange habit of making sure she was breathing before I could go back to sleep, as if the whole thing was going to be ripped out from under me.

Certainly the full on commitment of the next step was weighing on me. Searching for a solid and sure feeling that she is the one for me, our progress plateaued with a comfortable living situation. A subtle thing happened one day that gave me a gentle nudge. As she stood on the sidewalk reaching up to water a hanging basket of flowers, I drove past on my way to Home Depot. A sudden feeling came over me that held a solid glimpse into the future. In a moment of introspection, I couldn't imagine myself without her. It stuck with me to this day.

Firmly in the good graces of a local contractor named Baxter, I enjoyed a solid job and reputation redeveloping the old Bethlehem steel property. The superintendent was well established in the company, as well as his presence at Bethlehem steel. Henry was well connected having spent nearly his entire career working there for Baxter. We nearly got every project there, as Henry was held in high regard by the developer. I was never one to socialize with upper management, Henry was an exception. He took a liking to me and my skill as an operator. He would prove to be a valued friend and a great example of being true to yourself. He had a no-nonsense way about him, yet he was quick witted and full of humor. He would say just what was on his mind and didn't hold anything back for fear of repercussion. I truly admired that and felt a great comfort with him knowing it was all genuine.

Being a people pleaser I was in awe of his ability to be himself. I could see that his way was the only way to live but I was too fearful, needing approval from everyone to offset my disapproval of myself. It wasn't long and I gained top status with him. I always got the best jobs and he kept me working even when things were slow. During one of these slow periods, we picked up a little job to keep us going for a couple weeks. It turned out to be a life changing event. The job was a simple retaining wall to secure a section of railroad. It was a pleasant change from the normal difficult work we do. After establishing a solid base for the foundation, we constructed the wall with large concrete blocks that needed my machine to lift them. Normally we had the same crew and worked well together. Coming into work one day I noticed we had another laborer. His name is Jorge and I hadn't seen him in a while. He was a good worker and had a light hearted personality. When I got a break I went over and talked with him. He wasn't his usual self and I could tell that something major was bothering him. He opened up to me that he had an aggressive form of skin cancer and it had spread throughout his body. It was awkward for me but his honest and sincere way put me at ease.

Although the content and circumstances were entirely different from the operator that inspired my career, the results were even more driving and inspired. Almost like a deathbed confession, he went on to give me his most valuable advice. He said with certainty in his eyes, "Don't wait". Don't put things off, don't think you have more time or that you will get to it someday. Do it now, because this is all there is and all we can count on. My head was in a spin, as if I had just been given news that my time is up. I got back in my machine and resumed my duties. Something very strange happened then that defied all previous experience. As I set the blocks in place I noticed a vivid perfection, as if I was seeing it, not doing it. It was as if I was stunned right out of my own skin. Awe struck, I continued the process being caught in this strange awareness of some other world. Trying to make sense of it, I started becoming uncomfortable and fear set in. My hands continued to move with precision and the blocks placed with perfection. The effect faded in a short while and one thought ruled my whole world with explosive determination. I have to propose to Katie and I have to do it ASAP. As if I was late for my own wedding, I headed straight to the jeweler after work. Knowing it would have to happen at the Shanty, I began to formulate a plan. And as luck would have it Jake Kaligis was playing there Thursday night only two days away. I put the rush on the ring and somehow, they pulled it off. Sure in my steps it all came together without a hitch.

Knowing her gentle heart was with me, certainty rang true in my heart and gave me the courage to say yes to love. Sitting in the dining area with the band playing in the background my heart gained a few extra beats. She finally went to the bathroom and I raced to put my plan in motion.

Free Bird

The great thing about a marriage proposal is people are only too happy to help. With the key to the castle, I first spoke to Jake and he agreed to give me the mic at a suitable time. Then I turned to a woman and her husband seated in the perfect place at the bar and she couldn't say yes fast enough. Then back to my seat without notice. Here we go, as I casually asked if she wanted to find a seat at the bar. The husband and wife faded into the background as we claimed the only open seats. The edge of my seat felt like the edge of a cliff as the moment approached. With only the rough outline of what to say, Jake paused and looked my way. I stepped in with both feet, all eyes were on me as he handed me the mic. Certainly not relaxed, but determined, I laid out how we met and how I came to know she was the one for me. Kneeling to her smiling face the crowd erupted in applause as she said yes.

Eighteen months after she first graced my presence, she agreed that I was worthy of her love. What could be more important than that, I thought. Her gentle and kind way gave me real safety. In her casual glances, I could see love's reflection calling me to see what she sees. Unwavering her love was never denied me. Unthinkable, could that ever change. She was and is a perfect reflection of something that was in me that I was unaware of.

Excitement filled the air as we planned our wedding. Date set, for a year later my responsible pace to my crown jewel continued. Without much experience in relationships, I still knew at some level that this wasn't a typical one. We have this foundation of tranquility that did not give way to drama. Somehow, we stayed consistent at home and in public. It wasn't so much with physical displays that represented our bond but a quiet agreement. Spending time together was never a chore but a relaxing comfort. I know what she gave me. It was a constant reminder that I was wanted. Truly she opened the door to my own acceptance of myself. Our wedding day was a resounding success and characterized by many to be one of the best. Surrounded by family and friends we stepped into the rest of our lives together.

Settling in, my life took on new meaning as a husband and stepfather. It wasn't easy with the kids, as I never felt that I was in a responsible position. The father was still very much involved, so my part was largely a supportive role. Katie would struggle at times with the shared custody, hearing joyful accounts of their fun with her ex who is married to her former best friend. I tried to point her to the reality that things aren't always as they seem. It was during these difficulties she also struggled with feelings of not being good enough.

Hers were always short lived and she returned to relative happiness. For me it seemed more difficult and my feelings of joy were short lived with longer periods of difficulty. As Coda and therapy faded away, Eckart led the way in my search for peace. Still taking the medication for anxiety and depression I began to see the downside. Yes, it had a numbing effect on my fears but it also numbed me to all my feelings. No matter, at last, my life had all the promise that life could offer. At thirty-nine years old I had by all accounts the happy ending I desperately wanted. The loving wife and family, friendships, and a good job. Everything reflected well on me, yet the peace of that night was still elusive.

Echoes of the past remain

Knowing that Eckhart was legit and somehow came to experience sustained peace, I knew that within his teaching I will find all the answers I need. I continued listening and reading everything I could find and my understanding grew. I could talk about my dysfunction and why I feel like I do and how it's just conditioning. My thirst for the ultimate understanding grew even in the face of him saying that freedom is not found through intellectual understanding. I couldn't see any alternative and continued on as if I would be the exception.

No doubt my life has improved immensely. Every part of my life changed for the better. All from a seed planted many years prior did I find the motivation for real change. Surrounded by the fruits of my efforts, it did give me a sense of accomplishment and normalcy but the pull to find peace was ever present. There was still an avenue that I felt hadn't been fully realized yet.

Money was always important to me, feeling it held the promise of freedom. I was fortunate Katie was also good with money and together we made good decisions and were still able to have things we wanted. Work for me was about to change direction again. Sitting at the top of my field, I began to be unsatisfied with my income. As luck would have it, while attending a union dinner dance, I stumbled on an opportunity for a job on a pipeline project.

Free Bird

Gas pipeline construction was considered the highest paying and best work in our trade. Vastly different from previous work I had done. Starting out, I relied heavily on my ability to run the machine and soaked up their unique way of doing things the best I could. It was definitely the most challenging type of work, and I loved it. It really took me to the edge of my capability, requiring maximum skill and creativity. Wild and free was the energy on a pipeline. No matter what humble financial situation you were in. If you made a name on the pipeline, it's like you hit the lottery. It was booming when I got my chance and soon offers came in to travel to other jobs. I was lucky to be offered jobs that I could drive to and I started building a new reputation.

Katie's banking job was eliminated after a bank takeover, and after repeatedly turning down pipeline jobs that took me away from home, we decided to try it. The kids had graduated high school and we were free to travel. The money was good with the pipeline but the downside is it's all consuming, with the minimum amount of hours worked being 10 hours a day six days a week. A foreman that I had worked for before was also climbing the ladder of popularity and was able to secure me a key position on a very good job in northern New Jersey. Only two hours from the house we were able to get home for one night a week. It was a great adventure for both of us and we really enjoyed it.

From there, we settled in back home with by far my best year financially. It was at this time that I decided I was going to try and get off the medication. It really didn't seem to do anything anymore and I started feeling like a zombie. Never one to take baby steps, I weaned off it within a month. Navigating several ill side effects, I found myself suffering from insomnia. It got worse and after going three days without sleep I went to the doctor and she prescribed me some sleeping pills. Full of side effects themselves I did the best I could, determined to stay away from the psych drugs. Spring came with another great job offer in New Jersey. Too far to drive we planned to stay in our previously bought camper. The day came to move the camper and my buddy was going to move it for me as I didn't have a truck big enough yet. My anxiety was in the red as we had difficulty getting the brakes to work. I was so worked up I told him to back it back in and I'm not going. He calmly diagnosed the problem and we were good to go. It was at this point that I knew I was going to have to go back on the drugs. My job simply doesn't allow for having that kind of reaction to something so small.

It was about a year later that I had another important realization. All the while, I continued to listen to Eckhart, and I even attended one of his talks in New York. I had given thousands of hours to his teaching and I could hear his voice in my head. Unfortunately, his wasn't the only voice; I had my own, and it was full of disruptive commentary having to do with my many shortcomings. Although he alluded to the fact that the self that I think I am is what stands in the way of real peace. Somehow it didn't really click for me what needed to be let go of. I guess I figured with enough understanding I would just add peace to my personalized sense of self and live happily ever after. Well, for whatever reason it all became clear to me and I simply wasn't ready for something that extreme and my progress seemed to plateau after that and even regress. Even on the meds I had an incident at work, not work related but it landed me in the hospital with a diagnosis of a panic attack and a recommendation to increase my meds. Embarrassed and set back, I felt lost in my quest for peace. Almost letting go of the idea it kind of took a back seat for a few years as the memory of that night started to seem more like a dream than a possibility. Though peace hadn't found my heart, I had gained a much different viewpoint of the world. Having more compassion for dysfunction in people around me, knowing it's just the result of past conditioning. Somehow this didn't soften the voice in my head though.

It's now 2015 and my pipeline skills are on full display and well known. It seemed like work just fell in my lap. Not only did I hear from respected pipeliners that I was one of the best but I started to believe it myself. I think this positive vibe reopened the door that maybe lasting peace is possible. The following year came with some uncertainty as work was slow to start. One well timed phone call and I landed a good job in the Hudson Valley on a good crew. We stayed in the same campground as in 2011 the first time we traveled. I had more downtime than usual and I recommitted myself in the search for peace. Although I still had difficulty in my social skills, I was quite open and direct at work. With this confidence combined with my skill, I was able to win over many foreman's and inspectors. Real connection without my work to back me up was still awkward and uncomfortable. I was able to find a level of worthiness in my life, but it was completely reliant on how good I was or how pretty my wife is or my car and so on. So my mood fluctuated like the wind. One thing I loved about Eckhart was that he was well studied in other wise teachings. So even though I stuck with him, I learned about many others and developed a well-rounded understanding of the human condition and how it may be transcended. Another reality check to give perspective. Although I had learned a great deal from Eckhart and many others, I didn't feel any closer to a quiet mind.

A growing thought increased its importance as another good job came to an end. I have to get off these meds. It became painfully obvious that the only reason I take them is to avoid the side effects of quitting. I did a bunch of research online and laid out a very strict weaning schedule that would last three months and supplements to help with the side effects. I was so eager to get started I cut my dose before the end of the job. It definitely wasn't easy with brain zaps and sleepless nights, but I did it. Just that alone gave me new hope for the future, knowing that at least it will be all me and not some lifeless ghost.

Onward and upward, another good job found its way to me shortly after I was completely off the drugs. So here we go, real life test. One good thing, they were all people I had worked with before so going in I didn't have to prove myself. I could definitely feel the increased emotions, but it was tolerable and I was quickly able to get in the swing. It turned out to be one of my favorite jobs. Lots of humor and hard work and I was able to perform as well as ever. I couldn't have dreamed I would be doing this well in such a short time. Before this job was over, I already had my next one lined up. Leaving on a high, I started my next job with a full head of steam. A funny thing happened, about this time. I started having issues with my throat. It started to get dry and I would get hoarse and have difficulty talking. At first a slight nuisance, then it started to wear on me. And out of the blue, for no reason at all, I fell into anxiety and depression. Completely without cause, my work was doing great, and they loved me. Puzzled with a little less wind in my sails, I carried on with growing concern. I saw a doctor for my throat and he said acid reflux, wrote me a script and I took a heavy dose for three months with no relief. Meanwhile, work had become a chore instead of a joy, and I really started to doubt myself. On top of that, my foreman looked to me for part of his job and I started redlining in the stress department. Amplifying it even more, my sleep started to really suffer. Half in a daze I just kept going with no end in sight.

Still getting by I began to only do my work and it wasn't long before my foreman was let go. It was a big job, so we were all reassigned to other crews. It was at this point that I noticed something peculiar. A coworker named Evan seemed to, by complete chance, end up wherever I was. A dozer hand that I had met in 2014 was suddenly everywhere I went. That was fine with me because he was a joy to work with. Always full of humor and good vibes, Evan was the center of attention. I continued my struggles but at least now I had a good crew to take some of the stress away. I remember a conversation I had with Evan as we scoped out a difficult section we had to deal with. I opened up a little about what I had been dealing with and he had quite a different view of it than I did. I said in a meek and tired voice that I had this throat issue and somehow I've got myself in a real jam. I elaborated on how I viewed my performance on this job. I said starting out I was a force and quickly was designated the lead hoe hand, just meaning I would do the more difficult work. I explained that slowly, as the clouds rolled in, I lost confidence and my work suffered. The next thing I know, the other operator started gaining confidence and pulled even with me. Evan said, in his usual Evan way. That's not what happened. In three words, he summed it up. Iron sharpens iron. First he said he didn't notice any difference in my performance and the other guy, who was used to not having to work at that level, focused and tightened his game up. Iron sharpens iron. Turns out it's in the Bible, pointing to how we lift each other through inspiring heights. His insight didn't right my ship, but I started to see him in a different light.

Typically frowned upon and almost unheard of, I asked for a week off to go on vacation. We had booked a cruise for late fall in the Eastern Caribbean with some friends of ours. So many years of avoiding any time off, I started to ease up on thoughts of conformity or financial consequences. In a major funk, I thought this will be a great way to snap out of it. I couldn't have been more wrong. Not only did it not get better, but it took a turn for the worse. My wife was the only one who had a clue as I was quite gifted at hiding my feelings after a lifetime of practice. I became so debilitated it was difficult to carry on a conversation. Between my ailing throat and awkward social skills, I kept quiet most of the time to avoid any suspicion of my state of mind. One day in particular was horrible as some concern and confusion entered the eyes of my friends. I just pawned it off as throat issues as they listened with concern. The same day we gathered for a group photo by a ship's photographer on a beautiful staircase. In a demented and self defeating mindset, I purchased the photo as a record of the worst day of my life.

Returning home, things didn't improve much and of course I had to lie to the guys at work about how good a time I had. You could almost say my whole life was a lie, trying to cover up the fact that I'm not good enough. Trying to hide it with skill and cars and of course a beautiful and loving wife. And now money, my latest venture in creating self worth was showing signs of failure also. Money is a difficult lesson to learn because it can always whisper in your ear and say it's just not enough yet. If that analogy were true, then wouldn't I have experienced some gain in self-worth? The wisdom teachings that rang in my head may not have given me peace, but they did show me an ever-increasing realization where peace can't be found. And I suppose that's all they can do. Teachers can share their path to peace to inspire hope, but they all know that it was very specific to their particular needs and none would say they did it.

I had scheduled an endoscope procedure with a gastroenterologist in hopes of getting to the bottom of my throat issue. He said that my throat looked in good shape to my relief, and that I had a small hiatal hernia and the presence of a bacteria in my stomach called H pylori. He wasn't that concerned about the bacteria, saying that half the population has it without issue. Even so, he saw it as a potential cause in light of the fact acid-reducing meds didn't do anything for me. He prescribed antibiotics and sent me on my way.

Now, it's Christmas time and we were fortunate to get about a week and a half off from work. Pipeline work can be crazy, and it's entirely possible to have worked straight through and even on Christmas Day. Not that I was in the spirit, still struggling with depression. But the findings from the procedure did give me a glimmer of hope that a.) it wasn't a grim life ending discovery and b.) maybe these drugs will take it all away.

Free Bird

New Year's Resurrection

It's New Year's Eve 2017. By this time Katie and I weren't much for parties or staying out till midnight. We decided to just have a quiet dinner and drinks at a favorite Bar and Grill we frequented. Not that she wouldn't have been up for more, but I wasn't in a very good state of mind. We noticed a couple we knew sitting at the other end of the bar. The woman was a memory care specialist that had a leading role in the operations of a nearby facility. My Mother was suffering from Alzheimer's disease and her condition was worsening. The lady came over to chat and of course asked about my mom. She was only too happy to share her wealth of experience. The next thing I know we are in a very in depth discussion unlike any we had before. She really came with compassion and empathy. As we continued, I noticed myself starting to feel emotional. Perfectly natural of course, but for me, it wasn't. So gifted I was at hiding that the slow progression of my mom's disease hadn't caused a single tear to fall from my eyes.

After living away from home for 30 years, our relationship though never lovingly close, drifted further apart. She gave me every ounce of what she could, but having self worth issues of her own, she couldn't give what she didn't have. After her condition settled in, we became even more distant. Through the years, she showed her love the only way she knew how. Through doing things for us kids we knew she cared and there was nothing she wouldn't do. I witnessed her struggle with self worth, seemingly even more bottled up than I was. An insight developed as her condition worsened. She lost her memory of how to do things, but also slowly lost the memory of herself. All the accolades from the past, as well as any grievance towards others or herself, faded from memory. Someone once said that unless you become like little children, you cannot enter the Kingdom of heaven. Though unable to function in the world much like a child, I had never seen my Mother more happy. Always wanting a hug and saying she loved me, she openly gave affection and loving support. She didn't transcend fear completely. Much like a child, she would fear childish things. It further confirmed to me what Eckhart said about the personalized sense of self causing all the trouble. The visits with her during this time were the most treasured and also brought to mind the occasions in my early life when this side of her would pop out. It really solidified my viewpoint that she was innocent and free underneath the dark thoughts of conditioning that gripped her much of her life.

By this point in our conversation at the bar my emotions started to overrun my ability to stop them. With watering eyes, I leaned over and whispered to Katie, we have to go. Rushing out tears started to stream down my face and I asked her to drive. Straight home as I started to feel like I was going to explode. Fighting with everything I had to stay composed, losing the battle tear by tear. Now in the kitchen trying to explain like an injured child with no relief in sight. Pacing with almost hysterical crying. I felt confused and clueless to what was happening. And then, like a light switch, I was catapulted back in time 20 years, almost to the day that I had first felt emotion so intensely. Oh my God, I muttered out. It's happening again. What, she said? With a worried look. My breathing hyper knowing I'm on a ride that won't stop. What do I do? Enters my mind as before. I just have to let it happen echoes in my head as I feel overwhelming intensity overcome my resistance.

As if I was frozen in time, stopping dead in my tracks, my world was transformed from hell to heaven once more. My very first thought carried the weight of 20 years of searching. In a very clear and vivid realization. I thought to myself, there is no way I could have ever gotten myself here. The contrast, so great, it defied all description. You could say it was pure love, but that didn't hold the slightest reflection of what it was. Marveling and in awe, I looked outside to see the stars holding my safety in their light. Everything was full and called out with gentle kindness and complete acceptance. In awe, I sat on the couch with love in my heart.

Having longed so desperately for this, and feeling that I could do anything, I had the thought of searching deep within myself for the truth. The Kingdom is within, so the saying goes. Not like I hadn't tried this sort of thing before, but this time however I seem to have the ability to really do it. I sat still with my eyes closed and somehow knew the path to the Kingdom, like a trip to the grocery store. Progress was fast as I descended into my depths. And like a cold bucket of water in the face, I was ambushed by this ball of fear jumping out at me and it snapped me right back where I started. It was like I was trying to run a roadblock and was quickly apprehended and sentenced to one night of fear. Yes, moments ago I was in the most blissful state and now there was this edge of fear mixed in. Certainly not back to my normal state, yet not entirely comfortable, I headed up to bed. Really not getting into detail with Katie, as if I could anyway. She settled in with really no idea what just happened. Still feeling this tinge of fear, I lay there confused about its presence. Eventually falling asleep and New Year's Day came in with a brand new me. The fear, completely gone and I was loving life. It seemed that this was going to last this time and it came with grand imaginings of monumental significance.

Things like the second coming came to mind and my mouth was busy dealing out all the wisdom I had learned to that point. My wife is now meeting someone she had been married to for over 13 years for the first time. She was great and would sit and listen to me blabber on until I would see tears start to roll down her face. She quickly started to get tired of it, yet still she would attempt to listen. Yep, this was it. I'm like Eckhart now. Where would you like me to start speaking? Oh, I had it all. A complete lack of fear, conviction with authority, and a suitcase full of wisdom.

The next day brought another great adventure, back to work. Such joy in just driving a car, feeling a witness to a perfect Symphony. I glide into work in harmony and complete safety. The job had suffered a setback with an environmental issue and it had gotten shut down till further notice. Many workers fled to other jobs fearing it may get shut down completely. Evan and I stayed, and it turned out to be a great decision. We would meet every morning in the yard and were required to stay for two hours. Then we were free to go home with full pay. Arriving, I found a good spot and settled in. Evan was stationed over to my right and soon gave me a call to ask if I needed anything at the store. I said how about some chapstick, and he snickered and drove off. Of course I need the chapstick because of all the talking I was doing. He got back and pulled up alongside me and handed me the chapstick with his usual wit and humor. He said something to the effect that chapstick wasn't exactly a fitting ask for someone who's supposed to be a seasoned pipeliner, while he's sitting there drinking a latte.

He then went on to speak about his time off and family gatherings. He mentions some issues his daughter was having and the advice he gave her and I couldn't believe what I was hearing. It was as if I was listening to a great sage and it blew me away. I express this to him and he gives me this look and says, are you stroking me? I said no and elaborated a bit on why his advice was so good. It's like he didn't even understand how he came to it or why it was so good. The next thing I knew, I was sitting in his truck. And so it began. Every day we would sit in his truck and in the truest sense we encapsulated the meaning of iron sharpens iron. Expanding our horizons, we contemplated the mysteries of life. Of course I had an inexhaustible desire to talk in this manner and could have sat there all day, every day. Evan had a more balanced approach and after two hours, he was off to other things. Evan's wisdom was certainly an eye opener for me, and our relationship would only grow stronger from there. But another surprise was waiting in the wings on YouTube. I still had a great love for

Eckhart's teaching, but I felt a pull to expand my scope of understanding. A couple weeks prior I brushed across a teacher named Mooji and thought he was interesting, but didn't spend much time there. I got home that day still yearning for more and looked him up again. His effect on me was completely different this time. I listened in disbelief how he effortlessly conveyed perfect sense in a clear message of truth. Fearlessly, he pointed to something he made seem so obvious. That was it. If I had free time, I listened to him and his message grew in my heart.

Aside from a keen awareness of real wisdom, I also was blessed with a big increase in intellectual abilities. Able to swiftly and precisely deal with any situation. I got to the bottom of an ongoing problem with my wife's 401K that had lasted for six years in a matter of a couple hours. It was unfixable, but I was able to find the point of origin. It wasn't that I had a sudden increase in new information. It was a huge boost in clarity of what I already possessed. Normally my mind would filter all of my life experience through past experiences combined with any emotions I was feeling at the time. By the time the information was put into action, its effectiveness was considerably reduced. This newly developed ability was the result of a direct relationship with life. There was no middleman so to speak. It was clear and immediate action. Without even realizing it, the culprit of an age-old problem was revealed.

In ancient texts, to modern day wisdom, there is the concept of the separation. The day that humanity fell from grace. Could it be something so trivial and automated as this so-called middleman? Just a simple process of gathering all past experience as a foundation to judge any interaction. And of course all of this past experience is charged with emotional trauma heavily biased to avoid a repeat. So now anything that looks, sounds, smells, tastes or feels like a traumatic experience from the past, you will automatically see the present situation through the filter of past experience. Seems OK, right? Using past experience to avoid a repeat. Not touching a flame or walking out in front of a car, it's very useful. But what about a mother that had an extremely bad day at work and lost her job. Leaving her hopelessly in the grip of fear for the future of her and her daughter? Driving home lost in endless scenarios of doom for her and her daughter's future, she then wipes away the tears before entering the house. Now with the Mother fully composed later that night. The child rushes downstairs and says Mommy, I flushed the toilet and there's water running all over the floor and down the stairs. Like a flash she runs upstairs to stop the water, witnessing the unbelievable mess that will surely cost thousands. Now the innocent child stands behind her wanting to help as the Mother is flooded with thoughts of financial ruin and despair. Then turns to the child that's tugging on her dress and explodes in anger, releasing a toxic mix of fear and disregard. The child goes running in tears taking on the whole thing. Feeling that what was done was so unforgivable that the most important figure in the child's life cut me down as unworthy.

This is the viewpoint of a child that hasn't developed reasoning skills yet and internalizes it as a fact of unworthiness. I wish I could say that this sort of thing is rare and that it wouldn't have a lasting effect. How many experiences like this would it take for a child to develop a feeling of unworthiness? Innocent and naive of reason, there is no defense that can stop the child's fall into the conclusion that I am not good enough. From there, it could even morph into the inability to use the upstairs bathroom. There is no end to the destructive force it can have once internalized. Thirty years later, house shopping to start a family. And she will only consider houses with a single floor so there is no upstairs bathroom. There are likely thousands of experiences more or less destructive, and they all have varying degrees of impact on how we view the present moment. Is this a reliable source to effectively navigate life? It most certainly is not. Yet here we are doing just that. By some miracle I find myself released from this automated way of moving through life. Only then was I able to see how debilitating the normal way is. I didn't realize the mechanics of it at the time. All I knew was that I felt fantastic, full of energy and sharp as a tack. I wasn't graced with understanding outside my own exposure to things. I just had crystal clear access to what I did have without the influence of the middleman.

Evan would prove to be invaluable to me. His gentle and unassuming way opened me up to his well received guidance. Rarely tipping his hand, I developed a sense that he was much more than he let on. Always just out of reach of my understanding. Yet always there the moment I needed him. I was not blind to the miracle that he represented, but I wasn't able to grasp it. Little things he said slowly opened my eyes, like waking from a dream. He played his part so well he didn't even know himself. That's what really puzzled me. One moment he's giving me a glimpse of God in his voice, the next having no idea what he just said. Our moments together were priceless and would carry me forward to all the changes ahead. Slowly our connection pulled away, along with the peace in my heart. Things happened during this time that could only be divine intervention. And it would propel me to my next level of understanding. With anything in life, the greater the joy, the greater the payment, and I paid the price for this miracle. The pain of contracting back into the old ways was difficult, but with a newfound awareness I was led in new directions and developed an ever expanding scope to carry me to the next level. With each step, paid for in full.

Everyone's process in life is different and sending you off thinking my path would somehow work for you would be a mistake. The only thing that truly matters is your being open to your own process. Allowing life to lean you in the right direction. Ultimately, life here is all about the development of appreciation. The value you have for life dictates your whole experience. The more value, the more vibrantly life reflects that value back to you. How it's reflected back will always be a mystery. The essence of it is a clear message from your heart, because your heart is what brings about your whole life experience. This is why it's so important to find the love that's already there within. Firstly, you must begin to look at yourself with kinder eyes. Open that door to the possibility that feeling not enough inside, doesn't make it so.

Start to allow kindness towards the reflection in the mirror. Open yourself to the freedom of a willing heart. One who knows blame has no place in life, only learning. We all are born into this world innocent, and that never changes. We just come to believe it does through conditioning and life experience. All part of it. Without falling into darkness, so to speak, we could never appreciate the light. So if life has dealt you some tough life experiences, then all the brighter that light will shine.

Free Bird

The end of the road

The momentum and circumstances in my life right now are truly staggering. Over these next chapters I will attempt to give you the best description I can. There were many key things that happened after the New Year's Eve resurrection, till the day peace came calling. My only reason to write this is to inspire and bring to light the truth and the nature of life. Ultimately, this is a love story and even as I write this, it continues to unfold. I will give a summary of the events that I experienced to open this door to love and important insights.

The peace that came on New Year's Eve filled me with New Hope and direction. All manner of new possibilities arose and my eyes began to open to the presence of divine action. The harsh reality of peace leaving me started to be realized after three months and after 4 1/2 it left me completely. What didn't leave was my desire for it. It catapulted me to greater determination and a sense that I will do anything to get there. Anything, turned out to be a lot.

Firstly, I fell into A Course in Miracles. It truly is an unbelievable gift to humanity and it captured my heart. No doubt this book, A Course in Miracles is channeled from divine source. It opened my eyes to so much and brought meaning to the experiences I've had. I read with absolute attention to every word, knowing it is truly a look into reality and our place in it. Eckhart and Moogi stayed with me, but for a while it was ACIM dominating my time. I was in awe of the quality of writing and its crystal clear message of forgiveness. I won't go into detail as it's not for everyone. If you feel called to it and find it's very different and sometimes extreme viewpoints appealing then you will know it's for you. The main thing in each of our processes is, they are all tailor made to our specific needs and with an open mind and willing heart the doors will open.

After a year of daily reading and going to meetings and best of all, connecting with people, I started searching once again. There was a woman living in Spain that caught my eye. A spiritual teacher that had an outlook on life that appealed to me. She spoke about getting aligned with life and how life would give you everything you need if you flow with it. It's funny looking back, but that's exactly what happened to me, although I didn't see it that way. I was just following my heart wherever it took me and there is the real secret. Somehow I was doing it without even knowing it. She would turn out to be a very important part of my process, and one that in the depths of despair, would give me a glimmer of hope in an otherwise dark and hopeless situation.

Eventually I reached out to her with a request for a session. She responded quickly and we met on Skype. It was an absolute delight meeting her. She displayed a very positive vibe and a volume of insights. She was very intuitive and quickly we hit it off. Relating on many levels, our roles of teacher and student melted away and it was just two people connecting on a very deep and inspiring level. As usual in life, it turned out to be very different than

Free Bird

I imagined. The idea was for me to spend time with a teacher and open myself to her teaching. In a way, that did happen, but there was a twist that I never saw coming.

After our wonderful 2 1/2 hour session going well past the allotted time. She then directed me to the secondary part of her services which was energy healing. I noticed on her site that she did that, but it certainly wasn't what I was drawn to. She instructed me to lie down on the bed after we hung up and relax. She said I may feel some sensations in my chest and that I would know when she was done. It lasted maybe 40 minutes and I would say there was a very relaxing effect and there may have been some other sensations, but I was more concerned about my homework and doing the things she said to do. Later that night there was a nice follow up e-mail with further instructions about drinking plenty of water and that the effect of the energy healing may take a day or two to kick in. OK, off to bed and the next day I awoke to something I would not have thought possible. Peace, straight up feeling the way I did with the other experiences.

What the heck is going on here? I mean, yes, I was open to something that I didn't really understand, but this, how? No matter, I was back and I just loved it. Work was a delight as I just killed it with my skill level and socially I was better than ever. I got back to her with a follow-up e-mail that expressed my deepest gratitude and awe of her ability. She was so happy about it she asked if she could use my e-mail as a review on her website. I was aware that it was unlikely to last, even so, I just enjoyed every minute. Sure enough, six days in it faded out. One very important insight came from it, and it would prove to be the only one that was irrefutable and hung with me through the trials ahead. The fact is, there is only one way something like this could happen being that we are over 1000 miles apart. And that is we are connected somehow. And if that's true. Then it must be true for everyone. Of course, she was gifted at her craft and it also requires an open recipient, but nonetheless this is quite a realization. Furthermore, all spiritual teachings point to the fact that we are all connected, and a step further, we are one.

The nature of my process was relatively slow at first. Once an openness for change developed, I set sail for a better life. Over the span of twenty years I came to a much softer view towards myself and the world around me. Driven to find peace in my heart, no stone was unturned. If I were to emphasize my greatest asset in this journey, it would be willingness. Willingness in my heart to let go and openness in my mind to see things differently. These qualities are truly all that's necessary. I was able to develop and attain all that the world promised to give me my worth. Not only by traditional means but also the alluring spiritual path of understanding. This search could easily have taken my last days. Time is a wonderful thing to allow for the beautiful discovery within each one of us. Yet it can also be used entirely in the search to make whole, rather than the discovery that holiness is our truth without conditions. Time carries no promise of tomorrow; only this moment contains the possibility of freedom.

Free Bird

The experience of energy healing gave me a boost for my next adventure in the Peruvian jungle of Pucallpa Peru. Ayahuasca was my next step in this process and it was a very big one that had far reaching effects. Some, very very good, and some I wouldn't have chosen in a million years. This is the nature of giving yourself fully to the realization of the truth. It can be extreme, no doubt, but will also cut like a knife through the dark clouds of deception. Certainly the path to freedom is unique for everyone, yet willingness in the heart and an open mind is the key to every door. There is a hidden jewel in the feeling of unworthiness and that is the ability to step away. When you teeter on a weak feeling of self importance, it's much easier to let go of rigid beliefs. As my readiness for change developed, life presented a reflective pathway. In the clouds of a limited awareness, it all seemed a bit random and chaotic at times. Now I see beauty and perfection in my whole life that inspires awe.

As we step into these unprecedented times of change. Know that it's a reflection of our collective call for freedom. We are collectively tipping the scales of our life experience here from a fear-based survival energy to love and prosperity. It's picking up speed and there will likely be turbulence until balance is reached and stabilized. The old isn't going to let go without a fight. Truly though the only reality this battle has is within each one of us. You needn't concern yourself with anything that's happening outside of you. Within holds the key to everything. Life holds up the perfect reflection of your inner state no matter whether you think the world is the problem or you are. If you think the world is the problem then you are of the mindset that turning the heat off in the house will fix the ailing refrigerator. Your experience in life depends solely on your inner state of alignment. Open to see your beauty within and your life experience will be one of joy and goodwill.

Getting back to my process. I ended up in a nine day ayahuasca retreat that slammed me, lifted me and everything in between. I experienced hell like I could never have imagined and also heaven. I walked out of there missing parts of myself and gained everything that was dear to my heart. The ability to give myself fully to everyone around me was more than just a gift. It resonated with every fiber of my being and I was going to take it as far as humanly possible.

During the retreat and for weeks after, time was experienced very differently for me. But not only me, the energies were so extreme, Katie also experienced time differently. It seemed an inconceivable amount of time passed during the retreat and for weeks after. I said to Katie, how long has the last week felt to you? At first she was puzzled that it had only been a week and then realized what I was pointing to. She said it felt like a month or more. For me it was inconceivable how much time I felt had passed. Having only the time that I've experienced in my life to compare. The estimation was in the thousands of years.

Onward and upward or at least I hoped. Quickly I connected with people all around me everywhere I went. I began going back to the ACIM meetings. I soon started my own meeting with the emphasis on real connection and understanding. Not so much on deciphering the text, but connecting with the people in the group and sharing experiences of triumphs and setbacks. All in the compassionate pursuit of coming together as a group and helping each other. At the same time, I discovered my ability to write. It wasn't great, but it had some real flair to it and it was the beginning of an opening to what you see now. My ability to process things was also greatly enhanced and opened more doors and possibilities. After a couple months had gone by I noticed the peace starting to fade as before.

A couple more months went by and slowly I reverted back to the old me. And finally one night I crashed far below anything I could imagine. I lay there in bed that night and this horrific feeling came over me. At first I resisted. But then it just became too much. The only thing I knew to do was to focus my attention on my breath. After a rough night, I awoke the next morning to a feeling of dread. If there was ever a time in my life that I needed God, it was now. All that I loved and wanted in life was gone. Nothing had any sense to it. No greater victim there ever was. Why? How could my good intentions be so harshly cast aside like nothing at all? Unrelenting, it continued day after day. What could be the point of life? All that I believed in my depth lay in ruins. No hope. No love for anything, just survival. I finally pushed myself to go back to work. And that was met with uncertainty for something I could nearly do with my eyes closed. I found myself unable to make decisions or perform at any reasonable semblance of my normal ability. Struggle was an understatement. For the first time in my career, my reputation was a hindrance rather than an asset.

Free Bird

What could be the purpose of such a destruction? Is it finally true that life has no meaning and it's all just a fluke? Everything is random and we vanish like dust in the wind. My whole focus came down to finding relief from this God awful feeling. Another session with the spiritual teacher from Spain had no effect. Supplements filled the shelf to no success. Aside from the horrible feeling, there was one other very noticeable thing that brought to light something unknown till now. Like a tongue investigating new dental work, my mind was continuously searching for something that was no longer there. My sense of self. It wasn't until then that I realized there was a continuous mind activity to reference my central feeling of who I am. Now there was nothing to find. You might think, Oh! well, it must be the ego has gone. No, the ego is not the bundle of thoughts that have been nurtured and cared for to be me. My beliefs that were instilled in me of lack and unworthiness or that I am this or that. No, the ego is a survival mechanism that is activated by trauma in childhood. In essence, the ego is a cry for love. As innocence and a pure heart are subjected to the harsh reality of fear and judgment, survival becomes the meaning of life. No longer does a free spirit feel safe to be, express feelings and explore the wonders of life. The world becomes dangerous and a struggle. The pure light of awareness recedes beneath a protective wall of fear. A child's mind has no defense or reason. Completely open and defenseless, the cuts are deep and life changing. The smallest thing to an adult is soul shattering to an innocent child.

Free Bird

We have grown used to a baby screaming in terror as we rock them and try to ease their pain. We don't realize just how traumatic it truly is for them, or for us. These scars are deep, and they rule our lives even when reasoning and understanding are present. Because the survival mechanism is already in place and running our entire life. The one thing that it protects you from more than anything is the original pain of the first cuts. We can travel the world and search for all manner of relief from feeling unworthy. But one thing we can never do is look at what lies underneath the protective layer. Here we cannot go. No, this is where unspeakable ugliness lives. This is where innocence was seen to be shameful and ugly. Where life became a pathway to death. What chance do we have born into a world filled with fear? We have only one. Beneath this shield of protection lives the truth of our loving hearts. How can I remove this protection that covers my hidden secret of darkness? The truth is, you can't. Your only direction once the shield is in place is simply to survive. Lowering the shield represents certain death. You have to remember this is all set up by a child's mind. There is no reasoning skills or understanding. We have this illusion that in adult life we are in control and that we know what's best. The fact is, we are not in control. Our minds are busy, and we strive to find peace and happiness.

We strive because we have the feeling something is missing or not right. It's a fruitless search that will never fill the void. Standing from the highest view of accomplishment will only give you the realization that there is no answer. Many have come to this. How many have fallen victim to drugs and suicide? Total failure at the height of success. History is full of overwhelming evidence. So obvious, who could argue? So what is the answer? There is only one - willingness. Willingness to let go of thinking you know what's best. Willingness to see we are all in the same boat and there is nowhere to point the finger. And most of all, willingness to open the door to self love. To start looking in the mirror with compassion and understanding. The path to freedom is not an easy path, but it is well worth it. Everyone's path is different. There is only one common element in those that know freedom and that is willingness. Somewhere, somehow their hearts became willing and this willingness will be met with absolute success. We all have the same opportunity. Life has you in every way. If you want more of the same, that's very easy, here you go. Try to live in relative comfort, surrender nothing and have a few good days and bad and horrible. That's life, right? It may be normal, but it's definitely not the fullness of life.

OK, back to my situation. I certainly wouldn't have chosen this, that's a fact. And this is exactly why you have to let go of thinking you're right. That you know the way. How could you? You are trying to negotiate life with blinders on. We gravitate toward comfort. We didn't become dysfunctional in a comfortable way and it's not going to be comfortable letting it go. That's all it really is, letting go. We are not going to let go of something we think we are. Nothing new here, it's been talked to death in spiritual circles. The trouble is, knowing what needs done is not doing what needs done. The accumulation of spiritual language is completely irrelevant to becoming free. It's common for sure. That was a large part of my process. If I can just find that one last key to open the box. The key is willingness. I could never have put together that what was happening was the best thing for me. I would have said you are insane. I would have said that I feel completely betrayed, abandoned and left all alone.

There is one key component that is missing now in the ego dynamic. My personalized sense of self. It's basically a collection of experiences that get colored with beliefs. I'm this, I'm that. I'm good at this and horrible at that. A whole storehouse of me. Until mine disappeared, or at least the connection to the memories. I still had the memories, they just no longer felt like home. Until this happened I didn't realize there is a constant movement by the mind referencing this collection to keep it established. Why in the world would we want to do that? Very simply, we do it because what we truly are was traumatized and rejected so severely that we had no choice but to be something that was more deserving of love. Because what I am is unworthy. Of course it's true. The most precious people in my life showed me how undeserving I am. I will earn their love. I will. How though? By being somebody else.

Through these very difficult four years I tried everything. I even broke down and tried psych drugs again, to no avail. It was just a very gradual climb to some sense of normalcy. I could never quite close the door on the reality of divine presents. In my darkest hours I could throw doubt on everything, save one. The energy healing experience, I could not doubt. So although I stopped searching, I held one experience to the side and marked it irrefutable. After a year or so, some semblance of my former ability started to appear but my experience of moving through life would never return to what it once was.

It's the end of June 2024 and I'm back in the swing of things better than ever. Two things never returned after the crash. My sense of self and my desire to search for peace. All I cared about was to find some comfort and stability after losing all sense of direction. What developed was a narrowing of my focus. It didn't come about through any conscious means. It developed out of sheer necessity. My saving grace was my work. It was all I had left. At first it was a curse because everyone had high expectations, especially me. And I was unable to live to my reputation. Slowly, I narrowed my focus on what gave me joy in the work. As it turns out, it was simply the graceful movements of the machine with my full attention. The movements became my focus with precise control. Forgetting about goals and any emphasis on production. And like a slowly unfolding miracle I met and surpassed all my previous skill levels. Focusing only on the quality of my work and not trying to take shortcuts. I was soon really enjoying my work continuously for the first time. Even when asked to do things that I would have previously found demeaning, I just put my head down and made the best of it. With only one goal in mind. Graceful action and quality of work.

Free Bird

Time to say hello and goodbye

It was a beautiful sunny day, July 19th 2024. Working on a little pipeline project in the middle of a landfill. And out of the clear blue sky, divine communication started. I was absolutely awestruck and I couldn't even wrap my head around it. No matter, because from that point on I was on a ride that not only didn't have any brakes, but there was no end to it. At first it was completely focused on getting me aligned properly and allowing Divinity to flow through me. It was very extreme for me, but slowly over less than two weeks, I let go and stood aside and was blown away by what I was able to do. I was already considered the best and now I was doing things I thought were impossible.

At the same time, something else came to be known. Time was no longer something I experienced in any normal way. Life became enriched to the point it was full. It was, and is a feeling of wholeness that transcends time in a way that makes, at times, a day seem like weeks, months and in some cases, years. And in the most extreme, at times over the past year, I had no sense that could conceive of the amount of time passed. It's a very strange thing, living in time and yet free of it. The beginning phase led to peace that's never left me. It's not like it's something added. Quite the contrary, something left. The tortuous voice in my head left me during this initial balancing, and that was that. I went to a music festival on August 4th 2024 and was blown away how beautiful and joyful it was. Such a vivid quality to everything and I was so loving it and appreciative, it just melted my heart. Like everything after first contact, I wasn't given any time to relax and enjoy before things would move in directions I could never have dreamed.

Something caught my attention in my e-mail. It was an Eckhart Tolle retreat in Greece starting in the middle of September. At first, it was a mild attraction, and then the next thing I know I'm trying to book it as a surprise to my wife as a 20-year wedding anniversary vacation. The date was August 10th and to my disappointment there were no spots left. Oh well, keep moving. The next morning it's Sunday, my only day off. Looking through my e-mail I see something I knew was a sign for action. It said a few spots left for the Eckart retreat and I immediately asked Katie what she thought and she was all for it. It wasn't easy but by the end of the day we were booked. The accommodations turned out to be the more difficult. But by this time in my acclamation to this new reality, I knew if this is meant to be, it will be. And sure enough, a month before the retreat started, we were locked in. Hold on because this thing is just getting started and where it goes holds no value for my comfort or what I think is best.

We booked a few excursions and set out in preparation. At this point, I hadn't said a word to anyone about the constant communication, not even Katie. It was just too extreme, and I wouldn't know what to say. My mental processes were quick and precise, moving through things with ease. Even picking out clothes was a breeze. I picked out new wardrobes for each of us nearly as fast as I could walk through the store. Things just caught my eye. Not everything looked good on, but before you knew it we walked out with a bag full of clothes and they all looked awesome.

Also, what started happening at this time was I started writing and it was very high quality. And here is the kicker, it was 100% channeled. I would get the sense of something to write, always very early in the morning, and go downstairs. At first it was a little slow, learning to be still and allow the words to come, but once I got the hang of it, it flowed like water. The strange thing was reading it as it was written, just like I would read any other book. And Holy Mother was it impactful to me. What a strange experience writing something and learning from it at the same time. Being impacted to tears over and over again. There are still parts of it that will bring me to tears even now. In the end, it consisted of 143 poems and some other statements and general information.

Meanwhile, August 22 comes and suddenly I know this is the last job for me and I'm going to retire. It's not completely out of context. I had thought maybe the end of the year was a possibility but never would I have thought, in the middle of the season while work was booming. At this point, I knew my direction was held in divine action, but I didn't know just how extreme and unbelievable it was going to get. The following Friday was determined to be my last day. Something else became evident to me and that was how everyone started to treat me and see me. Of course, I just love connecting with everyone and getting to know them. The result was an outpouring of good vibes toward me. I could barely even carry my lunch box. My foreman decided he wasn't going to stay on past my last day, saying he didn't want to do it without me and took some time off.

The last day came and there was something else that was happening. As I parked the machine for the last time, the flame in my heart that burned so brightly for 37 years went out and I lost all taste for it. I couldn't wait for it to end and I never looked back. Unbeknownst to me, they planned a surprise retirement party for me at the job trailer. When I stepped out of the truck, to my surprise, it was onto a red carpet. There I stood being filmed, with expectations of me saying something. I carried on with a tribute to the local and how it gave me the opportunity to live my dream and thanked as many as I could. Damned if that video didn't make it on the local website as the most watched post of all time. Just spreading the love was my only intention and life just sends it back tenfold. Most certainly not all roses, though. Oh no, most definitely not. Love steered this ship with absolute determination and nothing was going to stand in its way. Not that I didn't try. The following Tuesday, the 3rd of September I drove to the main office, signed the papers and said my goodbyes.

While all this was happening my mother's health took a turn for the worse and was put in Hospice. We went to visit the Saturday following my last day of work and she was in major decline. Lying there, she was reduced to her coping technique of vocal humming sounds almost constantly. Awareness never left her though as she reached for my hand, eyes closed or not. I said my goodbyes to her, not knowing it was our last. I said to her as the tears rolled down, just let go, just let go. She let go of my hand in what I knew was her recognition of my words, and Katie and I returned home.

The next adventure starts as I'm looking online and a car catches my eye. It's a Mustang dark horse. Casual at first and then it just won't leave me alone. I brought it to Katie's attention and yes she likes it and always wanted one. But it's a lot of money and we have already spent a bundle on the vacation. No matter though, the next thing I know we're on our way to Newport, Rhode Island to look at a car a week before we leave for Greece. Something in me really wants this car, but I'm very cool about it and gave Katie the reins. You could say it was love at first sight for me, but I said to her it's fine whatever you decide, I'm good with. I knew if it was meant to be, it was a lock and just relaxed about it. She was warming to the idea and to sweeten the pot, it just came out of me. Well, why don't we just put it in your name? After all, you have always wanted a Mustang. That was it. She signed the papers. It sounds very manipulative I know, but this path was not paved with consideration for feelings and that became increasingly obvious. Then I drove it to our hotel where we planned to stay the night and head back the next day.

By now I had started letting her in on my new reality and of course she really wasn't able to come on board. But she would be kind and listen. One thing became very clear as this thing picked up speed. My comfort and those around me, are not a factor.

Direction, means, or money had no relevance. The only thing that dictated the speed and extremeness of my journey was my tolerance for it. And as it turns out, I had a very high tolerance, and I was about to find that out. A drive along the coast on a windy road and a beautiful sunset solidified my love for this car. There was something about the sound and vibration that just lit me up and I knew there was more to it than just a nice car.

Now, it's the day before take off September 10th. That's right, we are flying out of New York JFK on 9/11. Life has a unique way of putting me in situations and places that are deliberately contrary to the norm, with a side of humor. Well, there was nothing funny about the next day as I'm alerted by my sister that Hospice is saying any day now for my mom. In my previous life, a trip cancellation would have been expected by my family, but I knew and felt on a deep level this trip was of absolute importance and there was no way I was canceling.

As I pace around the house thinking of mom, the next morning, and last-minute details for the trip. I stand in the dining room staring at a picture Mom is in. And a very strange thing happened. Her eyes lit up, and I saw her in a whole new light. My whole life people said and I heard talk about how beautiful my mom is but I never really saw it. In that moment, I saw it very clearly and I said to Katie, wow my mom is beautiful. And a short time after that, my phone rang, and it was my sister. I knew instantly as I answered. And I said to her, I already know. And we struggled to talk and that was it. Mom passed as I looked in her eyes and I saw her beauty for the first time. It was one of life's little winks to the process of life. We were mother and son, and it wasn't my station to see her as a beautiful woman. The instant she passed, our relationship changed and her beauty was revealed to me.

Now I had to do the not-fun thing and say that I wasn't canceling the trip. There was talk of postponing it till we got back but life had other plans. She died on 9/11, two days after her birthday, and was buried on her and dad's anniversary 9/14/25, 62 years after their wedding day. One thing I want to establish before we step into the extremes to come. The past folds up behind me completely. What that means is I don't keep anything and am free of all of it. That sounds great right? Very healthy and what all the teachers say is the way. Yes, 100%. But what that experience is, looks like this. I carry a memory of all the incredible divine communication and amazing experiences, but no part of it do I get to use as a foundational support to draw on. So I only ever have right now, and that's it. The memories give me no comfort other than a reference for learning. I feel like Drew Barrymore on 50 first dates. I wake up and start all over again. But it's even more than that. I die to each moment and although I have premonitions of what's to come, it also holds no foundational value. Yes, the things I have written have come to pass with things in my own life and others, but it's the essence that is correct. I never know the particulars, like how, where or when. Even as far back as the New Year's resurrection, I started to see and know of things to come.

Free Bird

One very important thing happened at work on January 13th, 2018 at about 2:00 in the afternoon. After a communication of sorts, not as clear as it would come to be, but it was there. It was a kind of agreement to what I wanted, and I was all in. About that time it started to rain and the foreman called me and said wrap it up and go home. And away I went, clickety clack with my machine. Probably 20 minutes after my little communication, I was hit with communication that destroyed me right in my tracks. Communication of this sort had not really happened to me to this extreme before. It's a complete communication. In other words, you have a total experience, as if the message is a fact and that's how you experience it. Sure, that can be a very good thing, but it can also be the complete opposite.

The message was very sharp and clear. You will have to let her go. I burst into tears and became inconsolable. I poured myself into Evans truck, completely losing it. He tries to understand and I say I have to let Katie go. Of course he still doesn't quite understand and eventually says, if you keep talking like this you're going to end up in a psych ward. By 10:00 PM that night I was in the ER, consumed by fear and unable to talk. At about 11:00 PM, another communication came in the same way and said you caused all of this. Meaning the thoughts in my head. One by one a thought would come in trying to hold me and one by one I released them as my body shook for each. In the end I was free again and felt great. I started talking, and everything turned around. Protocol still held me to a three-day stay at, you guessed it, the psych ward. But it was beautiful and I actually enjoyed it. I quickly forgot about letting go of Katie and never gave it another thought. That premonition was about to surface and I would have bet my life it would never happen. Sure, free will is a real thing, but once you open the door to truth, nothing and no one will stop it from revealing itself. And anything that doesn't fit it's coming, is gone. Oh sure, I can resist it, but in truth, I'm just resisting myself and the truth is going to win out every time.

Two days before we left a small crack began to form in our relationship. My awareness had grown to a level that started to see things that irritated me. The little things that I began to notice were tiny and it never bothered me before. She would often want to know what I was doing on my cell phone. It never bothered me because I never had anything to hide. We had a very open and trusting relationship. I found myself very irritated and said to her that I was no longer going to put up with her asking me or limiting me or questioning me with places I go or people I see. I've given no reason for doubt and that is it. OK, I thought that was all there was to it.

We land in Athens and have a few hours to venture out on the evening of September 12th and we take an Uber to the Acropolis. We have a great time and explore all around it. One place keys my interest. As always, I will see something, and it just clicks and I move in that direction. It was an art gallery, and Inna Orlik is the artist. I was blown away by her paintings, especially Athena. She appeared to specialize in Greek gods, and Athena looked to be her crown jewel. One thing became perfectly clear to me. I could easily pick out divine works and also people with divinity flowing through them. There was a young man working and it was obvious to me he was flowing in the energy, and I later found out it was Inna's son. What I didn't realize is that I was just getting started with the amount of divine presence in Greece.

Back to the hotel and this is where things started happening that I couldn't believe. Almost out of nowhere, I break up with Katie, and at the same time, am crushed by what I'm doing. It's not entirely without context, as I started chatting with a girl online the second I said she couldn't ask me anymore what I was doing on my phone. How's that for irony? The chatting was nothing, and it stopped that night but somehow it got me to do the unthinkable. The thing about this process is, life is going to get me to move by any means possible. When I say life, what I really mean is Love, because that is what makes the world go round and makes everything possible. Love steers the ship according to what our hearts call for, and mine was wide open. And love was answering that openness with directions and experiences I could never have imagined.

The next morning we are on our way to the resort on the West Coast. The Tolle retreat made it easy for everyone to find transportation, and we were a few days early, so it was just three of us. A young man from DC joined us, and we chatted the whole way. When it comes to any spiritual conversation, I'm all in and so was he. That would become a recurring theme. I continuously connect with similar people with high energy, and that's only increased to a point of meeting people that defy logic with the abilities they have. A little like rolling back the curtain, but really all it is is my ever-expanding awareness. Stranger yet, with my heightened energy, Katie and I were good and continued on having a good time as if nothing happened. I would simply reframe it as we are best friends and will always be a part of each other's lives.

We arrive at the resort and I immediately loved the energy and people. This place would come to feel like home to me, far beyond any concept of home I had before. As I have mentioned before, the past folds up behind me in such a way that I'm not able to use it as a comfort in this very often extreme journey. What I am given for support though is numbers, music and little winks and synchronicities. The Angel numbers started some years back, but now they were on full display and very obvious. I would just suddenly look at a clock or phone and many other ways, see the number, know it was important, and look it up. And without fail, it would be relevant to whatever was going on at that moment. It didn't really give direction, more a confirmation that I was where I needed to be. It was a perpetual way for the divine to give me much-needed support. There was communication, but there is something about seeing it or hearing it that gave me comfort. Music also was very important. It was like that particular song was written just for me at the time I'm listening to it, and it was awesome. Unless you have experience with this, you likely won't relate.

The number 222 came to be a meaningful number. It was the room number at the hotel by the airport we stayed at. After check in at the resort we were handed the room key and then escorted to the room. Yep, you guessed it, the room number was 222. Sure, you could say coincidence. The odds of this are astronomical and it was no coincidence. It wasn't long before something else happened that caught me off guard. We went exploring and ended up in the reception area. We waited at the concierge desk to ask some questions, as she was finishing up helping someone else. She turned towards me, and our eyes met; it was like I was struck by her eyes. I immediately said to her, I've never seen so much light come through someone's eyes. She was impacted by it, and it set her back a bit. I would eventually come to know it was recognition of divine essence. Not understanding it for a long time, I assumed there was a romantic connection. That caused all manner of problems, but it had its purpose. I was left to learn a lot without any help, so that it would really be driven home. This was one of those lessons and it would be many months before I would come to learn it. And there was a very important reason it was left a mystery for so long. I often speak with a tone that this journey is about learning. It very much seems like it, but in truth, expanding awareness confirms with clarity. Discovery is the name of this game, and there could be no greater.

Evan was back in my life at this time, also and was huge for me here. Always being there at just the right time, and when I needed to do it on my own, he was unavailable. Evan was the one there for much of it, but I also would receive help in all manner of ways and from the most unlikely people. I came to know that if someone is telling me something, to listen up. And at the same time, the things I would say and do would be equally helpful to them. Soon, the resort and the people that worked there felt like home. I slept very little and wandered all around the place in the middle of the night. Often I would end up at reception talking to whoever was there. The vacation lasted 10 days, but very much like Peru, it was like time stopped, and allowed me to grow and discover I am meant to be here. This is my home and these are my people. Katie and I, though in turmoil, had the vacation of our lives. Till it was all said and done, we broke up 7 times and it was hell, leaving me in disbelief. I finally came to know there was no stopping it, and let her go, and it just crushed me. The saving grace of not carrying the past is, after I expressed all the emotions tied to breaking up with her, it was like it never happened and I was completely at peace. I fought with everything I had, but in the end I knew I had to let go to save endless suffering. Truly our love for each other is real and she gave me nothing but love. When it comes to the nature of this process there is a much larger picture that considers the betterment of the whole. Even this statement represents a kind of hierarchy that's not really there. Elevated energy simply moves towards the same. My change is just too extreme for us to cohabitate. It's been a rough road but we have come to a place of understanding and we support each other 100%.

Many incredible things happened in Greece. Heartfelt connections, and developing awareness to see and experience a world defying all conventional possibilities. The purpose of this book is to open the door to the fact that Divinity surrounds you, holds you and is you. You need only be open to it. Reality is far more than anything I can put into words. This can only be experienced for yourself. Come to know that you don't know. Humble is the way to freedom. Developing trust will lead to a willing heart, alive with direction.

This journey is not one of conceptual understanding. It's letting go of all of that to reveal what's already there. It's not a development, it's a discovery. The part of you that searches and needs to know, simply fades in the clarity of expanding awareness. There is absolutely nothing lost except the suffering of trying to be something you're not. Understandably, holding on to what you think you are, but it's what causes all your problems and makes you feel something is missing and not right. Giving up the idea you know what's best, opens the door for change. The best word to describe the process of awakening is strange and yet beautiful and awe inspiring. Willingness is your only part; willingness is the key that opens the door to freedom.

Free Bird

Finding my way

Maybe the hardest part of stepping into reality is letting go. One by one, the people in my old life left. Of course Katy was the hardest, but eventually I would have to let go of all. There is a kind of push-pull movement that happens along this path. There is a never-ceasing push for freedom and a pull from my past to stay the same. There are no shortcuts. I'm not able to avoid speaking and doing things differently. Any sort of dysfunction that went on in my relationships would no longer be acceptable. And it wasn't long before silence began to fall on my social life. Family being Ground Zero for dysfunction would be my greatest challenge and source of pain. And what better way to face and deal with it than moving right back in with my dad?

There are times I just have to chuckle a bit, looking back on how life threw me into the hornet's nest to deal with things. Even at that point of my life, having a much higher awareness level. There was still a tendency to think I didn't have anything to deal with; it was just them. Maybe that's the biggest and hardest lesson. It's only ever about you. The minute you start to look in the mirror for the source of the problem is also the moment the door opens to the answer. After all the change within myself, I somehow thought I was no longer subject to life reflecting things I need to deal with. Well, no, it's their dysfunction that's causing the issue. It may be true that I can no longer be in everyone's life. But it's equally true that we all deal with life the best we can, and there's no place for a finger to point.

Finding a balance between having boundaries for myself and giving others freedom to be as they are would prove to be difficult. One thing that really surprised me was how no one I knew saw freedom from the chains we place on ourselves as their number one goal. It became painfully clear that everyone I knew was willing to settle for survival. Finding the most comfortable life is a natural thing. Not just with humans, but all life. Change is painful, and given the choice, few would choose pain over comfort. That hits on a very important insight. The ones that find freedom are not focused on avoiding pain, their focus is on transcending pain. In a way, everyone is trying to do just that, but for the masses, how that's done is staying in the comfort zone of familiarity. Only when life brings you to extreme difficulty will there be an openness to change. We all encounter challenges, and it's here that opportunity knocks. You can run for cover and try to find comfort or finally say OK, what can I do because I'm willing to do anything to change the cycle of suffering. When this level of openness is reached, hang on. You are now on the path to freedom, and nothing will stop you. You are completely surrounded by divinity and will be supported in every way. This is not an easy path, definitely not, but it's well worth it.

September 27th 2024, I'm sitting in the Mustang that's now in my name. I set out with a car full of clothes wiping tears from my eyes and a heart full of what the hell just happened. By now it was quite clear I was on a ride that will not stop, and no matter what I think is coming, it won't even be close. There were two things to come that I was made Privy to. The first is that peace is coming, World Peace. Yes, the huge changes happening around the world is the beginning of a change that in the end, peace will be and love will rule. The second is that true love will find my heart. That little premonition would send me in every direction, filled with assumptions and even heartache. Yet with all that determination, not a single one of them took a step in my direction. It took time for me to understand, but I came to know I was off limits. No matter how perfect it seemed to be, there was no way anyone was going to come close to me, until one did. But we'll save that, because there is a whole lot of road between here and there.

At this point, I had no idea what to do or where to go, but faith was in my heart, and it showed me the way. Many of the lessons were quite difficult, and I would end up learning them in the most difficult way. I would later learn that it was necessary for full appreciation and value to reach my heart at the deepest level. Yes, that's been given me to have such love and appreciation for life and the lovely people that continue to come into my circle. But I pay for every bit of it. Every step was paid in full, no shortcuts. I certainly don't say this to garner any sympathy because it is well worth it. I say this, to point out very simply, this rule of life applies to everyone. You only receive what you are willing to pay for. There are no shortcuts in life, only the illusion there is. No one gets away with anything, no matter what you think or see. Karmic action is real and there is a perfect tally. You may think you have gotten away with something, but I promise you that this is not the case. At its most basic, it's simply cause and effect. What you send out comes back. Life mirrors what your heart calls for. Put out deceit and you shall receive it. Have only love in your heart and it will return tenfold. The only difference in my process is my heart pushed the fast-forward button and it kept me right at the peak of my tolerance for change. All that's really happening is the truth is coming out and it's not interested in comfort, gentleness, or popularity, only progress. This trek is not just about ascending to heights unknown, it's also to maintain the lower awareness for contextual contrast, resulting in the highest appreciation possible. In other words, rising from the ashes of hell to know the truth of heaven. Giving full appreciation and value to what we are creating, heaven on earth. Seems over the top, yet everyone has this same potential and will come to know it. Time for this is coming to an end. So yes, this is the big change happening right now that's been forecast for thousands of years.

After a week or so staying in hotels, I'm in the car driving back to my hometown to stay with my dad. This drive home felt very much the way it did when I left home over 37 years prior. I was full of wonder and excitement for what the future may bring. Arriving home, things were certainly somber. My mom, having just passed away 3 weeks ago, set the stage for some tough times for me and my dad in the weeks ahead. My mom's presence was evident at this time and definitely helped me get through it. The changes that came to me in January 1998 weren't really noticeable by my family. I would only spend maybe a few days at most visiting. Especially once Katie came into the picture. So, of course we were all just happy to see each other. There was one time Katie and I stayed for a couple of months for my work, but the bulk of my change wouldn't happen till many years after that, so there wasn't much contrast. This time, the change was immense, and after a couple of weeks, ripples formed into tsunamis. It was tough and I was minutes from packing my bags several times, but in the end we have a relationship now that's far better than it ever was. Every part of my journey has been rooting out every corner of darkness and bringing it to light. Where this was possible, bonds were strengthened, and where it wasn't, they fell away. It just happened naturally. I didn't decide anything; it just happened. Friends just stopped calling. I didn't have to say a word and family too. That took me a while to understand that no one was going to be in my life that I wasn't energetically compatible with. They either would rise to some level of compatibility or fall away. The best part is all the new people that continually come into my life.

There were two main things that I focused on after moving back home. One, getting the first book that I wrote published. It was well written and full of insights, but it turned out to be just for my growth and understanding. That took some months to burn out. I quickly became aware that if I struggle too much with something, there is a very good reason for it. It's not meant to be. The other thing that consumed me is this feeling inside that I need to find love. I joined dating sites, met girls on Facebook and in person, and all it ever was, was me chasing my tail. Truly, between my dad, the book, and chasing Love, I grew a lot and began to realize where importance was.

It's now early December 2024, and it seemed all my aspirations were just going down in flames. The book got put on a shelf, and love just became a cruel joke. It was at this point that I opened myself to the ever-present guidance within me. I simply said in a kind of surrendered and discouraged voice. What can I do? And like it was on a springboard just waiting for me. Fill your heart with love. It was during this time that I began to discover the wealth that was within me. Every time after that for anything or problem I got the same clear message. Fill your heart with love. Like a broken record, that's all I would get. It seemed at first that I was softening my views on everything and letting go of the fierceness that developed through all the trials and difficult letting go. But truly, what was happening was that love was starting to flow out into every part of me and all around me. So this has been my process from the start. I go through things that strengthen me to the point of fierceness, and then there is a tempering process of love coming in and balancing me.

With love at the helm again, the idea for this book came at some point in January 2025. The theme was relatability and inspiration. And I began to realize from a place of clarity that there was a lot more to my life than I ever realized while I was living it. Writing was slow at first, maybe an hour or two a day, but sometime in early April it took off, and it was 8 and even 12 hours a day till it was done. Or at least I thought. It turned out the last four chapters were for me once more. Just one more thing that I thought was something that it wasn't. Life was going to drive this home to me until I would lose all desire to want to know or even venture a guess on what the future will bring. This was definitely one of the hardest lessons. It got to the point I would be turned every which way and upside down until I let go of projecting what, where, or when and finally just flow with life, knowing it has my back. I had a relatively easy time from January to April. Of course, I say relatively, most certainly not normal. There is just no way I could write everything that's happened from July 19th till present day, which is June 18th, 2025. It's my aim to give the most inspirational, interesting and relatable information I can. These later chapters are definitely going to challenge the relatability part, but what's coming is coming and I feel it can be a help for the times ahead.

So here we go. During December of 2024, I started plans to go back to Greece, always knowing I would. December was a little tough as my direction was seen to be fruitless. I felt drawn to solidify my next trip to Greece. As soon as I pulled the trigger on the flight, I had a huge boost in confirmation of the right direction. Oftentimes guidance can be subtle and I have to take a step and then there will be a feeling of, yes this is right. It's given me a real sensitivity for direction. Direction can also come from anyone around me. The best advice may be heard from the most unlikely place if you are willing and open to hear it. Ultimately, everything works as one; whether you see it or not, it makes no difference to reality. The fact is there is complete support around all of us, always, but you have to open the door.

Free Bird

After making all the plans, I really started to feel in line with my path, and then the book. I guess you could say that I really started the new year taking steps on the right path and everything before was the end of all the wrong thoughts, ideas and directions. One thing to bring attention to is something that happened in the later part of March. A little thing at a place where I had some alterations done on some clothes for the Greece trip. I walk into the store to pick them up, and it's prom season. The shop is full of dresses, mothers & daughters. I stand at the counter ready to check out and look to my left. And I get hit, Pow! Similar to looking into the eyes of the concierge in Greece. It was the most beautiful thing I had ever seen. It was a long dress with sequins that just made it pop. Of course, by now I know this means something, but I just grabbed my stuff and went. I couldn't get it out of my head; it just wouldn't leave me alone. The next day, I called and had them set it aside. A couple of days later, I stopped in and bought it, knowing there was a reason, and then just had them store it. After going through everything I've gone through, it's not a stretch for me to think this is for the one love that will truly find my heart. That didn't stop me from imagining the two that I already had in mind fitting into it. Anyway, just a side note for later.

April is where things really started to pick up again. Some, very good and well, you know. With every difficult experience would follow expansion of awareness and clarity. The more difficult, the more expansion. April 6th turned out to be the most difficult. It was the only experience that I was given a heads up. I won't go into details about it, I'll just say that it was just pure survival. It took me

3 days to recover. Even Katie called me the next day, somehow intuitively knowing something happened. This experience opened the door for a lot more insight.

On April 12th, I came to a much higher state of consciousness, and of course without any prior knowledge it walked into open arms. Many things happened at this time, every day something significant and this day I felt a higher freedom come and it was a very welcome event. Little did I know I was going to need every ounce of it in Greece, which was fast approaching on April 25th. It's interesting how my expansion coincided with the start of the full moon cycle. It wasn't till afterwards did I see that my heightened freedom and the start of the full moon coincided.

There was a recurring theme that was present from the start of this ride. And that had to do with my safety. It would prove to be a difficult one to transcend. And I was given quite a bit of leeway on this. Little by little, it was proven again and again. I never even thought to actually put it to the test, but that didn't stop it from happening. The more I got comfortable with the Mustang, the more the envelope got pushed. All the way from deer to police, I had to be shown nothing could happen. So yeah, there were plenty of white knuckle days. The thing that was so hard is, and this includes everything, not just dangerous things. What you call for in your heart is what life will reflect back to you. My heart carries no ill intent and a genuine love for life so that's all I receive. It's not about what you do, it's what you feel when you are doing it. All the pesky things in life come as a reflection of what you are feeling and though there were times of discomfort, time after time, nothing contrary to my safety or well-being. Only if there was something I needed to learn would there be any friction, but even then, no consequences.

This will likely be a sticking point for many, but the thing is, I'm not here to talk you into anything. I'm only writing down the facts. Another hurdle I had to cross, is saying the most unbelievable things to people and not even batting an eye. That took time and to my surprise, it's all about my conviction and the energy I feel within. I can say things to people that a couple of years ago would have put me on the, that guy has lost it watch list. Sure, there are varying degrees of acceptance, but my message has stayed the same. And always I know if I'm saying something to someone, there is a reason. Often, I'm not privy to why, I just do it or say it. After that I walk away without concern. I see changes in the people around me. There are limitations according to their willingness, but I have seen positive changes. And now Greece, well, enjoy. These last three chapters are packed full of anything and everything.

Fate Finds it's Mark

April 24th 2025, I take off from the Buffalo airport headed for JFK. I have a 5-hour layover at JFK and enjoy that extra time exploring a bit. There's still this unceasing search for love, and wouldn't you know, I come across someone with potential. A beautiful girl that fits the dress size. After a bit of a cold opening, she warms up and we talk for some time. One thing that can give me the wrong idea is the energy that flows through me paves the way for a deep connection, whether they are available or not. So it always seems to me that the person is really into me. But as always, she very nicely says she has a boyfriend. There is always something and by now I know, just keep moving. But admittedly, there were a couple that I pushed past the edge of being appropriate. No matter though, none took a single step in my direction.

The flight from JFK to Greece got delayed and was eventually canceled altogether. Nothing like a flight cancellation to bring out the demons in people. The captain earned his money that day and security. Me, I just went with it. Eventually, over the next two days, everyone either got a refund or rerouted, except me. I stayed the course and just waited for the airline to give me what I paid for, a flight from JFK to Athens. That took three days. I put myself up at the TWA hotel right in the airport. I highly recommend a stay here; it's a very unique hotel, and I had a blast and met some awesome people.

Free Bird

My direction is always quite evident, and learning and strengthening are constant. I haven't touched on a lot of what it's like for me in this process, hour to hour and day-to-day. There are a lot of tears. Not really sad tears, mostly joyful, but some just come from how extreme the experience is and I won't really know why they come. It's always immediate. I don't or can't carry anything. It just comes out and then it's gone. I live everything to the fullest. Everyone I meet and everywhere I go, I'm all in. Every encounter, I give myself fully and I form lifetime relationships in hours to a few days.That's not a goal, it's just what happens. Of course, it's wonderful to be able to gel with and connect to everyone I meet. There was a lengthy learning process to bring a healthy balance to it. So many times, I would try to latch on to these encounters and hold them. Mostly, they are just meant for the one connection, and we go our separate ways. The ones that stay are easy; I don't have to give a lot of attention, it's just natural. And the brief encounters are wonderful, and we move on.

An inspiring insight has developed in this process, and that is there really is no letting go. There is just the experience of connection in all different ways. Once the initial response to hold on subsided, things became much easier and much more enjoyable. Love has us cradled in its arms, and if we allow, love will give us more than we could ever dream of. It would be some time before I would come to this and to be honest, this realization is happening as I write this. As I've said before, I learn from what I write. My learning and growth are represented in what I write, as I write. One lesson I learned at the TWA Hotel is walking with conviction and love in my heart opens all doors and no one questions it. There was a very-high end wedding that took place at TWA, and I attended the reception and the after-hours party without a single question. I, of course, was very respectful and didn't partake in any food or drinks, but there may be some confusion when they look at the pictures. The toast brought tears to my eyes, and it was wonderful. Ultimately, it's just love giving me the greatest experiences as I open myself more and more to its loving way.

I met another woman there that may end up being in my life for a long time. We just clicked and even considered more, but realized we weren't compatible in that way. Finally, my flight leaves for Athens very early, at 1:30 AM on the 28th. Originally, I planned a four-night stay in Athens, but I just rented my car, stayed close to the airport one night, and headed to the West Coast in the morning. It was so much fun having a feeling of freedom, on my own, and loving life. I stopped at the Corinth Canal. What a marvel that is. I recommend a look at that. I had great anticipation returning to the resort, the trip seemed to take forever. And yet, when I arrived, it seemed like I just left Athens. My experience of time, or really lack of, was very strange. Arriving there it was a teary-eyed reunion with one of my closest friends I made there. It was surreal, and it was just so awesome being back, and I wasn't going to waste a single moment of it. My plan was to stay two nights at the resort, and then I booked an Airbnb in the beautiful village nearby, where I planned to stay the rest of the month. Well, it wasn't long before I realized life didn't care about what I thought was going to happen. As if I already didn't know that. I was going to experience this at an extreme that eclipses everything to this point. For now, I just really enjoyed my time here. Taking every opportunity to meet new people. My heart ended up finding its mark in the spa this time. Specifically with one of the masseuses and an exercise trainer. We really made a deep connection, and it's just grown since. I did have the opportunity to explore the possibility that the one concierge was my one true love. I pushed to the edge of being appropriate, and she handled it like a real professional. She helped me realize we are not meant to be together, and that was that. I left there with a full heart of appreciation and some new friends.

Checking into the Airbnb, I noticed right away that I had already been here on my last trip, which was quite synchronistic. We had only spent a few hours here last year, and this is the one shop we visited that wasn't on Main Street. I had no idea it was also an Airbnb, and through a strange situation with my original booking, I ended up here, right where life wanted me. These people would prove to be some of my closest connections I made in Greece. We grew very close very quickly and on the third night of my stay they invited me to a family outing and it truly made me feel like I was a part of their family. It was just a perfect gathering with a beautiful sunset. And they even allowed me to join them in lighting a candle at this little church. So yes, my love for the Greek people just grew and grew. The beauty of their country was only eclipsed by the people.

Free Bird

1:30 AM that night, I woke up to the name Tribulation ringing in my head over and over. I'm told I need to go to Tribulation. There are people there I need to meet. This was a little different than normal. It was more insistent, probably because it was so far out of expectation. A bit begrudgingly, I started packing, knowing I may never return. It's 6:00 AM and I'm in my car and unbelievably, on a trip that would take 10 hours. When I took off, I didn't even know over half of it was on a ferry. Or that it wasn't even a village, it was a club. All I know is everything just got turned up a notch and it's just getting started. I had to pull over a few times and shut my eyes. After maybe one or two hours of sleep and a little too much to drink, I wasn't exactly fresh. I remember this being very hard for me. I was very disoriented and mentally dull. Certainly not the hardest thing I've been through, but it had a different spin on it. It was revealed to me that deception was going to be a big factor in the coming days. You might say, if there was a weak spot in my strength, it was being disoriented. Well guess what? The only way to grow strong in that area was to get overloaded with it.

Finding strength and maintaining faith in the face of what seemed at times an impossible situation was my life for some time to come, especially with things we take for granted, like GPS. The divine are in control of all electronics and Holy mother of God did they F with me. There is no telling how many extra miles I put on, but it wasn't long before I knew what the deal was. I just kept digging and my tolerance for it got stronger and stronger. When I finally pulled into Refina Port, I felt like I just finished a marathon blindfolded. Of course, that wasn't the end of it, oh no. Like a yo-

yo, I went here and there figuring out the ferry process and a place to stay overnight as the ferry left first thing in the morning. Every single step posed a hurdle to get past. Nothing came easy. The ticket process was vague and I had to redo it and then ended up paying almost double out of ignorance. Then of course all the hotels are booked. One thing that I always have in my favor though, is the kindness of the people. I got that room and lay my head on the pillow and awoke feeling like brand new. Where is life taking me now? I have no clue, but always I'm given assurance for each step with an ever growing sense that all is well.

All tucked away, my little car finds its place on the ferry. What an adventure this is. I didn't even know ferries like this existed. Holding over 1000 passengers and 200 vehicles, it advertises a speed of 67 miles an hour, and I believe it. Several hours later, I arrive. It's so strange having the sense that I'm right where I'm supposed to be and yet not have any clue why or what's to come. Rolling off the ferry, I set into exploration mode. I have an exciting feeling of freedom as I negotiated the winding mountain road leading from the port. Passing through a village I was amazed at the vista seen from the higher elevations. I wound my way down to a beautiful coved beach lined with businesses supporting beach life. As I roll past what looks to be a restaurant, I sense some kind of importance, but keep moving. I come to the end of the paved road where there is a very large building, and I'm thinking maybe this is the club called Tribulation. It looked closed, so I turned around and headed back. I passed the same place as before and again felt there was something important there, yet I still kept going. After a few 100 yards, I felt I needed to go back and see what's up.

Then I saw this beautiful house that was behind the restaurant, and parked the car. It really popped with traditional Greek colors. I walked along the walkway thinking how well done it looks. I see a couple of guys painting a shutter and ask them about the house. It turns out it's a hotel and I'm speaking to the owner. He says they will be open in two weeks. I asked if he could recommend a place to stay. He said yes, down home Suites by the port is the best choice. After a nice chat, I said thank you Lucas, and was on my way. As I was getting close to my destination, another place caught my eye. Catherine's holiday home. I thought, why not? So I stopped, and sure enough, a woman came out to greet me. She says she wouldn't be open for another week and pointed, saying, Down Home Suites is just up the road and very nice. If two competing hotels recommended this place, it must be good. As I pull in, I see clearly I'm at the right place. Shortly, I'm greeted by Nico and his wife Elizabeth.

On the path of fate, I set foot on this island. Unknown to me what lies ahead, clarity would come slow, and yet my path was rapid and extreme. As for the club tribulation, it of course, wasn't the real reason I came, and yet it did have its purpose. Through some in-depth talks with Nico and others, I learned of its contrary nature to the traditional Greek culture that I loved. I found myself consumed by what started as a minor irritation and grew to fury towards this imposing energy behind the club. It was here where my ever-deepening love for Greece reached new highs of appreciation. And yes, as always, there was a price to pay. With every expansion of awareness, there was an equal payment of difficulty that came with it. Yet this toll I speak of is not an outside force demanding payment. It's simply the strain of letting go of limitations and misconceptions. All of it is tailor-made for each willing soul. Tolerance for it is the only ceiling. Ease and comfort play no part in it. Often, its coming was unseen, swift, and unrelenting. Recovery would vary upon the severity. Some expansion was steady with moderate discomfort, and some held no description of how extreme the experience was and took days to recover from. Yet those experiences came with huge gains, and the pain of the process floated away like it never happened.

I have to admit some of the details of my journey I have difficulty sharing just because of the extreme nature. I have to weigh out whether it will be of any use to someone reading this. I will share this only because there is a relevance to it, insofar as taking life here for granted. It's quite amazing looking back at how life was able to put me in the perfect situation for me to react accordingly. As I said, I became overrun with feelings of disdain towards this opposing energy. So much so that I said I needed to go to the bathroom. As I entered the bathroom, communication came in that indeed, I was here to eliminate this darkness that was growing here. And then the rug was pulled right out from under me. In the process of somehow destroying the opposing force, I wouldn't make it. It hit hard, and it took me 15 minutes to pull myself together. Few face death as a fact and live to be given the great blessing of life regained. Walking out prepared for death, communication flooded back in, singing a very different tune of life. The divine presence that surrounds me is filled with sadness of having to do that, but what a blessing it is. I thought I couldn't get any more appreciative, but that experience was one of the sweetest I've ever had. Truly, you cannot know unless you go through it. Since my crash into the depths of hell in the spring of 2020. It's as if I was dropped from the sky, falling slowly at first, hitting every branch on the tree of appreciation. Not a single difficulty was spared me, but also not a single blessing of ever-expanding value for life. Truly, appreciation for life is the ultimate prize.

Nico and I would sit each morning after his chores and talk about life. Synchronicities would come to light in my path to meet him and his wife, Elizabeth. The two other places I stopped before coming here are family members. Out of well over 100 hotels, I stop at the two that are family to Nico, and this theme of synchronicity would continue. Now that the club thing came to a conclusion, I was wide open to explore the island. Nico made a nice little map and itinerary for me and away I went. Beauty covered my eyes wherever I looked. I visited historical landmarks and museums, but of course what I loved most were the people I met. I decided that I would only stay two nights instead of the three I planned. After buying my ferry ticket for the next day, I set out to view the beautiful sunset that everyone talked about. I parked the car where Nico told me to and wandered into the village on my way to the high church. As I walk through the village, I was taken aback a bit by how unique it is. It's a mix of shops, services, restaurants and also people's homes. It's like a maze of tight corridors with high walls never giving you a glimpse of where you actually are. As I wind my way through, I get the feeling at times I'm going to come to a dead end. But it never happens. Later, I was told there are no dead ends. Almost contrary at times I would have to travel down to find the path up to the high point above. Each pathway was paved in these precisely fitted flat stones and well-maintained. One thing that was ever present in Greek culture was their passion for the quality of work and their desire for kindness and respect for others.

Finally, I reached the summit at the high Church and what a view. After an hour or so of the most beautiful sunset I've ever seen, I make my way back down to the village. Walking out, I really start to get interested in the village and decide that before I leave on the ferry tomorrow, I'm going to come and explore further. As always, I only sleep 3 or 4 hours a night and it gives me a lot of extra time to explore. After my morning walk, Nico and Elizabeth show up and start their morning chores. Nico and I sit and talk again when he's done, and I tell him my plans. It still amazes me how quickly these relationships form. I've been there now, less than two days, and already I know I'm speaking to a real friend. I get all my things packed up and figured I would drop back for final goodbyes after my trip to the village. I parked at the same place I did last night, and off I went. I had a good three hours before I needed to get back, so no hurry. No clue where I was going. I take a different route in, and as I walked past this little shop. Pow! I get hit with this instant attraction to an outfit on the wall in this store. It was just like what happened to me with the dress back home. I walk in, and a very nice lady greets me. Of course, it turns out she knows Nico very well and has all the best to say about him and Elizabeth. So here I am again, staring at a woman's outfit, already knowing I'm going to buy it. I carry on exploring and something very unexpected starts to happen. I absolutely fell in love with this little village and the people in it. Shop to shop, I meet these wonderful people, and of course, they all know Nico and Elizabeth.

After a couple of hours, I came to see this beautiful little clothing shop. The colors, the energy is so inviting. I stroll in, scanning all the displays and decor. Not really paying attention, I see some movement in the corner of the shop. I'm maybe 10 feet away, and as I turn to look, a woman stands and turns around. She didn't know I was there, and I scared her half to death. She jumps, and I jump and she immediately runs to me and gives me the best hug ever. And there she is, like no other could. She jumped into my arms in that fateful moment. I immediately knew she is the one, and she did too, even more so than me, as it would turn out. Immediately, she had me sitting down as she brought me coffee and snacks. We spared no time getting to know each other, and with every stroke we fit perfectly together. She is very passionate about clothes and helping people look their best, and it wasn't long before she was eyeing me up for something new to wear. She quickly goes to work, and I'm in and out of that dressing room, having the best time, meeting her approval. I learned quickly she has a good sense of humor, and I lay it on her thick and she loves it. We laughed and played with each other for hours. We covered all the normal things, but we also went into the depths of each other's thoughts and beliefs. Step by step, we found ourselves on common ground. My ferry had long left, but my fairy tale was just getting started. Watching her interact with the customers, I was amazed. She gave them everything she had to make their experience the very best. They would leave there looking good, but even more so, feeling even better after Penny blessing their lives with her presence.

We were swept away on this fateful day, the 7th day of May. Our hearts found their own reflection, opening our life to a whole new direction. Love found its Mark in the most romantic way. Yet even here, in the glory of our love on full display, there would prove to be a heavy price to pay.

We spoke of things as if we had been together for months and even years. The kind of comfort and recognition reserved for only the fairest of tales. The synchronicities that would come to light would challenge even the most open-minded. First of which, of course, do the clothes fit? After some thought I say would you mind trying this outfit on? I wanted to see what it looks like. Only too obliging, she agrees. Even I, after all the divinity that surrounds me and knowing she is the one, could hardly believe how well it fit. She danced around with it to my delight, and I thought, wow, this is rolling out like a red carpet, giving me the green light to give her everything. I guess you could say this is where the slightest of cracks began to form. I say to her, it's yours and she says, Oh no, Mark, this was not purchased for me. I say, I think it was. She gently says no, this I cannot accept, it would not be appropriate. This was the beginning of my awareness that we each had our strengths and weaknesses. She was emotionally mature with a strong foundation of propriety and process. Her heart was wide open, and she fell hard into my arms. Even so, she would always speak her mind and give me clarity. I said to her, I'm so amazed at how you give your heart to everyone. She says in her soft yet very direct way, not everyone, Mark, not everyone. I could see there was an incredible depth to her. A maturity that I had not known. One little thing that I found so cute that she said. She asked me as we sat outside the shop. Do you mind if I smoke? I reply no, do you mind if I don't? She fires back, I don't know. She comes off as the most kind and loving person I had ever met, but she is no lightweight when it comes to awareness or wit. As it turns out, she was far more open and aware of our significance than I was at this point. Yes, I was most certainly aware conceptually she is the one, but with her, she felt it and knew it at the very depth of her being. And that would prove to be overwhelming for her in short order.

We finished out our day together, planning our future in some detail. She said things like she would teach me how to speak Greek and also how to cook. She had just started working at this place and went on and on about how much she loved the owners and how they hit it off. Suggesting that I hop a ferry to go and meet them on a neighboring island. Almost like meeting her parents, which is how I felt. She took her job very seriously and our plan was that we would spend tomorrow together until it was time to catch my ferry. Then I would return in three to four weeks to resume our time together. She wanted time to get the shop in perfect running order and get familiar with everything, including the people in the village. She possessed my same social ability, and even though she had only been there a couple of weeks and this was only her second day running the shop, she seemed to already know everyone. We said goodbye with an affectionate hug, and I'll see you tomorrow at 11 AM, when she opens the shop. I left there just beaming with excitement and a feeling of awe at what just happened. Of course, I was only too happy to lay out the events of the day to Nico and Elizabeth. Nico says humorously. Maybe don't buy another ferry ticket until you know for sure this time.

She closes her shop at 10:00 PM that day and I thought I would wait till 10:30 or so and go back to the village. It was such an interesting place, I wanted more. As I walked in, I drifted past her shop. It was dark as expected, but it did glow with fond memories. I zigzagged through the walkways until I came upon an interesting place still open. It was a restaurant, and it had a very alluring vibe to it. I walk in and turn the corner and guess who is sitting there at the first table, larger than life. She says Mark, in her lovely Greek accent. Please sit with us. She explains this is her friend that she worked with before she came to her new job. I could tell she had a few drinks and was a little out of sorts. She says to me, you look very handsome in the clothes you are wearing. Still wearing the same clothes she picked out, in my typical humor, I said thank you, a lovely lady picked them out for me today. Well, this is where the first sign of trouble began to show. The joy in her face left immediately with a look of horror. One thing I learned in Greek culture is they don't always recognize this sort of humor and tend to take it on face value. She did well with it earlier in the day but with some alcohol and what appeared to be a bit of an emotional state, she took it as some other lovely lady was picking out my clothes. I immediately saw the misunderstanding and said no, it's you, silly, I'm talking about you. Her face lit up again, but to be honest, she never really recovered after feeling the sting of it.

She then says to her friend that sat between her and I. Alex, could you please allow me to trade places with you so I can sit by Mark? Then she wants me to drink a shot with her. At first, I was a bit reluctant, but of course I really couldn't say no to someone so lovely as her. It was quite good, a mix of Greek liquor and honey called Rakomelo. Her emotional state started to be a little more obvious, and she excused herself, saying she needed to talk to the chef. They had previous interactions. Not surprising, she is very social and easily connects with people. I sat and talked with her friend for a while, and I could tell he was a quality friend to Penny. The restaurant owner then came over and introduced herself. Her name was Theo, a male name, and she was very engaging and interested in how I managed to end up in Greece. She made me feel like I was some long-lost family and so did the others she introduced me to. She offers me another shot at the bar, and I have to say I was really taken aback by the affection they all seem to have towards me. Giving me a hug, she said you are welcome here anytime. That really went straight to my heart, and the loving energy in this place was unlike any I had ever felt.

Penny began to struggle even more and started complaining about her heart beating out of her chest. She is by no means a weak or immature woman, and intuitively, I knew what was going on with her. The connection that was made, or maybe I should say discovered, between us comes with extreme emotions, and she was in the midst of it. Even though I knew what was going on, I wasn't overcome or affected like she was yet, and that's a big yet. It was decided that Alex would take her home, and we parted ways. I deliberately went a different direction to give her a rest. The place is a maze, as I've said. It wasn't 5 minutes, and we came face to face again. This happened two more times, and sure enough, we are parked very close to each other. One thing struck me that she said as we covered the last bit of the walk together. Alex, helping her along, I say to him in my usual humor. It's lucky for me you're a stand-up guy because you are twice my size. Penny looks me straight in the eye like she just snapped out of it and said. Mark, he is physically stronger, but not in the Soul Mark, not in the soul. Unknown to me at this time, she is far more open and intuitive about our connection and significance than I was. On an intellectual level, I was aware of our connection and why she was struggling, but on an energetic and emotional level, I was far from where she was. And I'm sure that didn't help her any. It would be weeks before I would come to understand better what was up with us. Sure, I knew a little bit about twin flames, but I really was ignorant of it for the most part.

That night, I sent a few supportive texts to help her feel more secure. I spent most of the morning visiting with Nico and

Elizabeth. Then I was off to meet with Penny. I honestly didn't know if I would buy another ferry ticket or just see how it goes. Often, I won't know till I need to, and when I got to the turn for the village or to the port, I knew today was the day I would leave and went and bought my ticket. I arrived first to her shop and she strolled in a couple minutes later. I could tell she had been through the wringer. But beautiful as ever, and she had her hair down like I had hoped, asking her the day before. Even though she had a rough night, it wasn't long, and we were right back in sync. We spent three more hours together and it was awesome. When we were together, our concerns just melted away, and we just naturally fell into comfort. Time for me to go, and we hug, and I love you crosses our lips for the first time. I'll always remember her shining smile, looking out the window as I walked away.

Free Bird

Mirrors of authenticity

Twin flame journeys are not easy. I'm not an expert, but I have read and spoken with true teachers. The ultimate purpose is not a romantic relationship. It's a spiritual journey of self-discovery. When twins meet, there is a deep recognition of your truth at a soul level. It's a little like sleeping comfortably in your world and someone dumps a bucket of cold water on you. We spend our life adapting to find relative comfort (but of course, never really feeling at home) and splash your hit with your true essence right in the face. Or I should say, in the eyes. The eyes are the windows and can quite literally impact you with divine recognition. In this mirrored experience of your authentic self, anything that's not true bubbles to the surface, and it's not fun. This discomfort will cause the one triggered to run and try to escape. Ultimately, there is no escape because at soul level, twins are the same soul expressed in form as feminine and masculine. Two separate bodies that are the same soul. As it turns out, at this point I am predominantly holding the feminine energy. All this means is, of the two of us, I transcended the hold of the masculine energy, meaning, mind dominance, and ego.

This set in motion an eventual meeting where the door is opened to a true soul union while in

form. No other experience is as fulfilling or extreme. Love of this magnitude is beyond where any words could hope to go. Twin flame unions are the foundation of the enormous energetic change that's happening in the world. In the truest sense, it's the embodiment of heaven on earth. This eruption of twin flame union is the catalyst that will bring peace everlasting. It may not look like heaven is knocking, but the fact is we are on the edge of a complete energetic shift from fear to love. It won't be without pain, but it's on rails and picking up speed.

There is a level of surrender that, once met, guiding forces will not be denied. This is my journey. I'm not being controlled, just very tightly guided. What I mean by this is I can step outside the box, so to speak, but it's very uncomfortable because it's against my own will at a higher awareness. This is why conceptual truth has only a relative truth, for that level of awareness. And also why this book is in continual flux. As I continue to expand, I see things clearer and want to change or add new perspectives. I wrote this with the pen, and then I go back and dictate it into a Word document. So there were many times I thought, it's done, and Nope. It's quite literally a race against my own expansion.

OK, back to Penny and I. For me, somehow, I just felt so calm and certain about it that I didn't consider there could be any trouble on the horizon. At this point, I didn't really understand the potential difficulties that can come from a twin flame meeting. That came to light in a very short time. After the ferry ride, I decided to just drive straight through to the West Coast and back to my Airbnb. I texted a few times, and we managed to hold things together with a text goodnight. I could already feel a bit of distance from her with the texting. I'm not really a fan of text, but that is how many prefer to communicate. The trouble with me is I love to write, and I love her, so you can imagine the potential trouble to come. The next day, I lay it on thick with the texting. I just felt so comfortable with everything; I didn't think of the difficulty she was having at the time. In my mind, the supportive and assuring things I wrote would put her at ease. Oops, that is not what happened. It sent her in a full reverse.

The next text I get from her is, Mark, I'm sorry, you misunderstand, we are just friends and that is all. I wish you the very best from the bottom of my heart. I fired back immediately and replied to you as well. She replied back with a heart. I come back with, if we are going to be friends, my name is spelled with a KKKK not a C. She laughed and said I could always write her in Greek then, as she's more adept at writing in Greek. So I used Google Translate to send her the same message in Greek. I knew the friend thing was BS and just carried on sharing things with her. Things I did during the day and people I met. She would only reply by attaching the let's be friends text she sent me last. This went on for a couple of days until she didn't respond at all. At the same time I would also share pictures and things on Messenger, but no response. Well, no good one anyway. Her next move was blocking me on Facebook. Strange though, if you're going to block somebody, why leave them continued access to your phone number? And this is how it was to be for a while. She wouldn't shut me out completely. The door was always left open a crack.

Free Bird

　　　Three nights go by, and the next thing I know, I'm back in my car on my way to the port and back to the island. It was a classic runner and chaser dynamic that can happen after Twins meet for the first time. Of course, I'm clueless about all that and go in guns blazing, so to speak. Funny thing, though, as the island came into sight, I felt calmer and the certainty returned. I stayed with Nico and Elizabeth again, and although they were taken back a bit with my return so soon, they were supportive and wished me the best. The next day came, and I waited till she would be open and have everything set up. By now, I was perfectly calm, and I walked in and just as before, she didn't hear me and walked out of the backroom, and surprised, she jumped again. Only not into my arms this time. Taken aback, she says, what are you doing here? I just calmly said I felt maybe we needed to talk a little. She was cold and distant at first, but I hung in there, and before you know it, the ice started to melt. She started to smile more, and the next thing I know she lets slip, my lovely Mark and I was back, baby! Then it was coffee and cookies and more clothes. She also helped me pick out some earrings for Elizabeth. Penny went to school in England and knew a bit about what English women liked and wanted me to let her know if Elizabeth liked the earrings. As I left there that day, she gave me a big smile and says, goodbye, my love.

　　　The thing about these twin flame relationships is, if there is anything that needs to be let go or transcended or whatever, it's going to happen no matter how much you try to hold it together. And we are both going to do things and say things that will blow this thing up. Here comes explosion number one. After I text her and say Elizabeth just loves the earrings, they were perfect. Penny replies back with, I'm so happy. It must have been about this time she unblocked me on Facebook. Good right? Wrong. Since she's seen it last, I had used our picture as my profile picture, and oh boy, did she not like that. I guess you could say there was a powder keg of emotions that she was dealing with, and the fuse just ran out. She was always respectful and never used any profanity, but she is a force, and you better believe I took down the picture. It was at this point the two opposing forces became clear. Something within me became energized and driven. As clear as any intention I had ever had, I was going to establish very clearly that I was not going to walk away, no matter what she threw at me. This ought to be good because by this time in my spiritual development, if you like. I knew there was nothing I couldn't do, and there was nothing anyone could do to change that. These lessons I learned came with a heavy price, but they have served me well. And there have been no experiences that are contrary to the truths I have learned.

Firstly, life can only reflect back to you what you hold in your heart. Calm in my heart, calm all around me. This is why, no matter who is near me, they will either come to my energy or they will leave. I have no fear of anyone. This translates to no one can bring any ill intent towards me and actually do anything harmful. I have no ill intent towards anyone, only love if they're open to it. Their openness will become obvious to me by how I interact with them. I established lifelong friendships and even family all over Greece in a very short time. Simply because my heart is full of love, and life reflects that back to me by moving me in the direction to meet all these wonderful people. And of course, meeting love itself. My direction was largely guided through divine communication, but there are and were many other guiding factors. I learned very quickly that if there was an obvious resistance in any direction it is because that's not the way. Even though at times it seemed like I had no choice, I was never controlled, only guided. With my expanded awareness, there was a very clear sense of direction with things to say and to do. And yet, to maintain the amazing sense of appreciation and value that developed, I also still had the sense of lower energy awareness or contracted awareness. So there are times I would feel discomfort in things I said or did, knowing it's not a normal interaction in the eyes of the world gripped by fear. The higher awareness would always end up paving the way, but it didn't mean there weren't a few detours. The first and clearest case of this was how I refused to let go of my wife. It took seven horrible and emotional breakups in two weeks to get me to let go. Finally, life presented a scenario that appeared to me as an out-of-character and heartless act on her part for me to let go. It wasn't true in the big picture, but it got me to leave her. The beautiful thing is, I really never left her, and we are still good friends today.

It was absolutely ridiculous to me that I broke up with my wife on our 20-year wedding anniversary vacation. And yet on a higher level, it was the greatest send-off I could imagine. It was made very clear to me that she was highly revered and, in time, would grow to no happiness above anything she had known before. It was very strange, but we had the best vacation of our lives together in the midst of the unthinkable. The difficult things that were said and done left me completely, and I would return to a loving and calm state. This is where I could see very clearly the effect I had all around me. To this day, she can't maintain any level of negativity if I'm there with her or anyone else. So after a breakup, in a short time, we were out having the time of our lives. It's taken many months of reinforcement, but I think she has come to know that I only want the very best for her and I will always be there to help her in any way.

The stage was set for Penny and I. It was the classic unlimited force versus an immovable object. I was about to meet my match. To this day, since the changes I've been through, she is the only one who was able to maintain a different energy for any length of time in my presence. It's no surprise to me now because, in essence, she has my same strength and soul, for that matter. From a higher perspective, this is a battle for balance. On a soul level, there is natural balance. Represented in form, impurities arise from conditioning. All that is not true must fall away for balance to be established. This is the Twin Flame journey. Each must balance the two polarities within. For her, it was the masculine energy that needed purification, and for me it was the feminine.

I'll never forget the look on her face as I stood quietly in the shop for our first faceoff. She comes wheeling out of the backroom on her way to the front of the store and right past me without missing a beat. The look she gave was a mix of surprise, love, anger, and pain all at the same time. I couldn't help but start laughing. The next thing she says is the owner said that I'm no longer welcome in the shop and I would have to leave. Nice try, but I just maintained my calm energy and avoided any sort of disagreement. Not once did I say anything to provoke her. I didn't point to any of her actions at all; I just stayed calm and certain of my objective. I began to look at clothes in the store as she was dealing with other customers. I was amazed at her ability to still maintain her loveliness towards them, although she was struggling with her normally keen eye for fashion. I snickered to myself a bit after seeing what she had them wearing. No worries, though; she was able to square them away before they left, and they look great. Meanwhile, she was really getting frustrated with me still being there, and it was around 7:30 in the evening. And out of the blue, she says, you have to go, I'm closing the shop. Now that is a big deal. For one, that day she was supposed to stay open till 9. And two, she has great integrity when it comes to responsibilities and proper etiquette. So it was quite obvious my presence had her emotionally off the rails. I said well, I would like to buy this shirt and that really set her off, as she was barely able to gather herself to make the transaction. In a quivering voice, she says, I need the tag, and as luck would have it, it's on the back of the collar, as I was wearing it. She comes over with a pair of scissors at my neck with hands shaking. And snip, she managed to get the tag off without any serious stab wounds. I leave, and round one is complete.

One thing I knew for sure is, it was pure emotion driving her discontent. I didn't exactly understand it, but I knew that even though I was upsetting her with my presence, I needed to establish to her that I was a consistent and calm presence, no matter what she threw at me. I texted her later that night to meet with me. A kind of olive branch, but to no avail. I rolled back in, early afternoon the next day, for Round 2. She laid it on immediately, saying that I need to go. Her frustration was reaching a boiling point, and she walked right out of the shop to find someone, anyone, to help her get me to leave. The village priest was walking by, and she was well acquainted with him. She pleaded her case with him, and he looked at me and then her, smiled, and walked away. Infuriated, she stormed back in and on the phone. The next thing she hands me the phone, and it's apparently one of the owners. The wife says I must go, and I politely say I'm just shopping and not causing any trouble, and next, it's the husband. If there was anything that I did that was somehow disrespectful, it was with these two lovely people. But it was not out of malice; it was ignorance. You see, a restaurant owner nearby that I trusted had told me at lunch that day that it was Penny who owned the shop, not the older couple from the neighboring island. Looking back now, I know Penny had way too much integrity to lie about it. In the moment, though, I just went with it, disregarded them, and hung up the phone. I sat down on the bench and continued my stay. Maintaining my peace was my only focus as she stormed about. She must have gotten through to this woman that I hadn't met before. She walked in, staggering and out of breath. She asked me, very uncomfortably, please leave. I say to her, I don't understand why she is so afraid of me? I then stood up and walked towards Penny and said the only off-color comment that I've ever said to her. I said that I could never be with a woman that is afraid of me. And in that moment, I looked in her eyes, and it wasn't fear I saw, it was pain, and I turned and walked out.

Really, at this point my whole perspective changed, and I wasn't planning on bothering her again. Having said that, I wasn't planning on splitting with my wife either, but that didn't change a thing. Intuitively, I knew there was purpose behind my actions. I had a strong sense that I needed to establish my stability and conviction in her eyes. Emotions like this are very strong, and I needed her to know I wouldn't run at the first sign of trouble. During the day's events with her, she did mention the police, and she may have even called them. I sat down that night and wrote a heartfelt letter and sent it to her as a text. It basically said that I had no wish to upset her and that I love you and want only the best for you. Also, I want you to know that I am here and will always be. I don't know what tomorrow will bring or whether I will come to see you again at the shop. I mean no harm, but I will do as I'm guided to do. She replies, the police are aware of you, and if you do, they will come. She blocked my number after that. So you see, yes, she was very emotional and uncomfortable not being in control of her life as she was probably very used to. But if she truly didn't want me in her life, she would have blocked me long before this.

I didn't know it at the time, but the things that we both had to deal with were the other one's strength. Life had completely destroyed me over the past several years, and I came to a place of surrender and peace. And that's exactly what she was meeting; a very difficult situation to break her control that she may surrender and allow life to guide her to peace. For me, to my great surprise, my heart was not open to love like she represented. I know she is the one beyond all doubt, but I didn't know it in my heart like she did. But oh boy, was that going to change. The next day, I strolled right back in there, fully prepared for anything. Knowing so long as I maintain peace, no ill intent and complete lack of fear, nothing harmful can come to me. So business as usual as she storms around, and it may be 1/2 hour or so until the police show up. There are three of them so she must have got them thinking I was a real threat. You could tell by the look on their face they were expecting something very different. I just sat there deciding on a pair of pants I tried on earlier. Eventually, when they got their bearings, they approached me with some questions. I say I'm just shopping, and she is upset with my being here, but I haven't done anything inappropriate, so I don't see a problem. Of course they have to follow procedure and ask if I would mind coming down to the station for a few questions. I readily agree and ask Penny if she would lay those pants away for me, and off we go. No cuffs or anything, I'm not under arrest. It's all very civil and friendly. But it did take a little while to win them over. At the station, I hit it off right away with the two younger ones that were just starting as police officers. I even showed them pictures of Penny and me, to show us in a different light. It wasn't long, and I had them laughing and having a good time. The Sarge was a cool customer, and it took some time, but even he was in good spirits when I left. I think what got him was when I said you must have really thought I was a threat, bringing 2 for backup. He's twice my size and he said with a gleam in his eye, do you think I would need backup? That set everyone off, and we laughed.

Poor Nico had to bring my passport from the hotel for the background check. He says to me as I'm using the police phone. Uh, Mark, is this the police number? I said yes, Nico, but it's fine and I'm sorry for the inconvenience. He had a nightmare story that he told me about a friend of his, and I think he was having some flashbacks. Moving on, I noticed a new player about the time Nico showed up. A very serious-looking cat, and he kind of lurked around, eyeing me up. The background check took a while, and eventually this dude pulled up a chair on the other side of the sergeant's desk, facing me. For context, there is one thing you have to understand. Because of the extreme nature of my process that I have been through and am still in, this little thing here with the police is so tiny, it doesn't even register on my radar as any kind of a threat. And who, I assume, is the captain, was going to find this out in short order. First, he tries to create a picture of me as some sort of menace to the village. Saying that I was disturbing the shop owners and being very disruptive. And of course, this is the farthest from the truth. I gave only love and support to them. Although there is one who might disagree. He then proceeded to stare me down and this is when he saw something that he had probably never seen. Total peace, completely void of fear. Straight away, he got up and walked out and I never saw him again.

This may be hard to grasp as yet, but truly, life cannot reflect anything back to you that is contrary to what is in your heart. There have not been any experiences I've had that are contrary to this fact. I was put through unimaginable extremes to drive this point home to me. If your heart is sending out only love, then only love will be your experience. A fearful heart will know fearful things. I said that this little thing didn't even register on my threat meter. The fact is, nothing does. Nothing comes to me that's threatening. The only power there is, that can come at you, is your own power. If I had bowed up and became confrontational then I would have met an opposing force. I learned this very important lesson from a dog just protecting its owner. I stared the dog down with fierceness, and the dog met my every move with the same, mirroring me. When I relaxed and let peace come, the dog lost interest and left. Penny is, like I said, the only one that has ever been able to bring a contrary energy back at me for an extended period of time. And that is because it's part of a divine process that transcends normal karmic activity. Like a moth to a flame, she was drawn to something that was burning her up. That's really the deeper meaning of twin flame, the one that burns up the illusions that surround you.

There were so many lessons and strengthening that took place before so that I could handle all of this. And as I took each step, I would be stressed to the limit of my tolerance and would emerge with more stability and clarity. One lesson that took a while is if you are completely uniform in your conviction, the world bows and gives you the right of way. Go at it half-heartedly and you will find obstacles. This is true of people, too. Own it completely, and they won't feel any reason to change it. So finally, my background check comes through, and I'm free to go. It was really a fun experience, especially with the younger officers. As I left, the note got serious. The Sergeant said, "do not go back into her shop." And of course I said no problem. The trouble is, I can never know for sure until I know it's time to go. But what I did know is that I didn't want to go back in there and bother her again. Back at the hotel, Nico and Elizabeth were relieved. No worries, I said, it's all good. Nico had this look of, here we go again. I said one thing you won't have to worry about is that I won't step over the line. As it turns out, the line is kind of a gray area. The next day, I still didn't feel to go yet, and Nico suggested I enjoy the island, go to the beach, and stay out of the village. Seemed like a good idea, so that's what I did. It was awesome and a nice change of pace.

That evening, I started to feel this will be my last night here and I'll leave tomorrow on the afternoon ferry. Then I thought, why not visit the village one more time and just stay clear of her shop. What could possibly go wrong? I went to all my favorite spots and said goodbye to a few I came to know well. And now it's time to go. I notice my feet are walking to the car on a walkway that passes her shop. I'm like, oh no, I don't think so. I can only imagine what you are thinking. Well, you must really want to go there, or you wouldn't be walking that way. And I would say yes and no. The part of me that is experiential, having the time of my life and yet also overwhelmed at times with the extremity of it all, is saying no way, I don't want to go there. And yet there is also a much higher awareness that's really steering the ship, and that ship is headed straight for her shop. I've been in this very situation so many times that I already knew. Yep, I'm going back into that shop. This time, though, much like splitting with Katie, I tried not to. I managed to actually walk past, but I didn't get far. It just became too uncomfortable and I turned and slowly walked back. Although I was uncomfortable with the idea of walking back in there, I was very clear on the fact that the things I do, say and write have real purpose behind them. And whether or not I was comfortable, it was going to happen.

At first, I stood outside the open door, watching her buzz back and forth, doing her work. She did one quick glance and saw it was me, and carried on like I wasn't there. Yep, that was close enough for me, and Nope, here we go. I walked in there like I was sneaking up on a tiger, which wasn't far off. She just kept doing her thing, and I did too. I reached the center of the shop, and she gave me one more quick glance and carried on. I stand there for a few minutes, and she comes up with a bunch of receipts in her hand. Puts her glasses on, and next the phone is in her other hand. Oh yeah, it all looks very convincing. Just a work call, nothing to see here. Of course, it's all in Greek, so I don't know what she's saying, but I know what she's doing. No matter, I stand my ground and sure enough, after 15 minutes, in walks the older policewoman that I met the day before. She is visibly upset and continually asks me why are you here? I say nothing, she says, I'm going to have to take you in. I gesture with my hand, let's go. She didn't immediately want to go, and continues to ask questions. I kept quiet and gestured again, knowing there was a purpose in this. From the first time I walked into her store, once she didn't want me there, I knew one thing that had to be established. I had to show her that I would not walk away from her easily, even at the cost of real consequences. Feelings that are this extreme force you to retreat for protection, and I needed to make it very clear that I was steadfast, calm, and stable. Even though she was a wreck emotionally, she needed this, and she was about to confirm it. Don't ask me how, but as I started to walk towards the door, I caught a glimpse of her face and in that seemingly small thing I saw a look of relief and acknowledgment. That yes, he will face the firing squad if need be. The officer followed my pace, and just as I was about to step out of the shop, Penny's voice rang out in Greek.

The officer said, wait here and walked back to talk with Penny. They carried on for five or 10 minutes and finally she walks back to me and says, you're free to go. She escorted me down the walkway for a while and continued to ask me why. I knew I could never satisfy her with an explanation, so I finally spoke up and just said I don't know. She says to me she doesn't love you, and I knew that was BS and didn't bother saying to her that she said she did. She didn't have to, though; it was all over her face and in her actions. As I walked back to my car, I had a real sense of mission accomplished, and I knew it was time to go. It was a sad goodbye with Nico and Elizabeth the next day, but I knew I would see them again. I also knew I would see Penny again and that we would come together. I didn't know how, when, or where, but I knew it would happen.

Free Bird

Welcome Home

Understanding isn't really part of the deal at this point. All I knew was that the things I said and did were necessary. That didn't shield me from feeling I went too far or not far enough. The higher awareness always had the upper hand though and gave me a sense of calm. For now, that is. Because, yep, you guessed it, now it's my turn. Looking at it now, it's interesting how our meeting was like a truth serum, and there is no escape. Arriving back at the Airbnb, I settled in, thinking, home sweet home. It's now May 17, and my emotions started to stir a bit. Still peaceful, yet as I walked around the village, there was definitely a change in the way I was seeing things. I just wrote it off as being tired, having driven through the night again, and getting little sleep. I got through the day and went to bed early. No matter though, I was up at midnight, and emotions started to stir, and I started feeling a real pull towards her. I know I can't go back. No, not yet anyway. So I do what I always do, I write. It definitely helps me see things more clearly. I started to have feelings a bit stronger than before, and my poise started to fade. Looking at the texts I sent her, there started to be a sense of desperation, and certainty turned to doubt. As soon as the first bakery opened, I was there getting my coffee. I set out on my usual walk that I love early morning and evening. Something's different, and it's not good. The beauty that captured my heart and gave me a sense of home was somehow gone. I began to realize it's not lack of sleep, it's an obvious change in how I was seeing things.

Free Bird

Well, it didn't take long to know why, and it was a very cold and sobering realization. Without her, life was meaningless. Walking back toward my room, my pace picked up as it started to get intense. Tears, already flowing as I put the key in the door and right to bed. I don't think I had ever felt such despair, and that's saying something. It's like I was backed into a corner with no way out. It was severe. The kind of severe that catching my breath became an issue. It was a kind of forced surrender that I didn't see coming, and suddenly I'm in a fight for my life. I felt this huge physical sensation of release, and I knew then exactly what was happening. My heart opened to love like I had never known before. Her essence filled my heart, and her face was crystal clear as her voice soothed my soul. My energy returned in a way that took my breath away. What is this as the tears streamed down? It was in this moment that I knew what Penny felt and why she ran. And I couldn't imagine how difficult it must have been for her to have me not able to match her feelings. It was so obvious in the pictures we took together. She was consistent in every picture, full of love, and then there's me, looking like I'm only half interested. This really blew me away. I never considered even for a second that maybe I was the one running and not her. Even as I write this, I can't believe it. It makes perfect sense, though. Yes, it appeared she was running, but she always left a little path open until it just became too much. I would show up at her shop, but not with my heart, and she knew it.

In the big picture, we gave each other exactly what we each needed. But at that time, all I could see was how I tortured her, and

I felt so sorry. I wrote that to her in a text, but it fell on deaf ears as I was still blocked, and rightfully so. Ultimately, it's quite irrelevant who did what and why. This thing is on the rails of a divine process, and my comfort or hers is not the prime objective. In the middle of it, though, I looked for anything that could give me some sort of clarity or confirmation. Early the next morning came with a total change in direction. Rather than spend my remaining time at the Airbnb. I suddenly found myself booking a 10-night stay at the resort that captured my heart and opened the door to my love for Greece. This place gave me a real feeling of home, and I knew this is just what I needed. I said goodbye to my lovely host and off I went. It wasn't far, so I figured to see her soon.

    I rolled up to the familiar guard post at the entrance with a real sense of, this is going to be great. I'm already picturing myself reconnecting with people that felt like my closest family members. Boy, was I about to get the rug pulled out from under me again. It just never ceased to amaze me how, no matter what I assumed or imagined, it was going to be totally different. As I pull up, ah, yes, I have a reservation. I'm sorry, sir, I don't see anything here. Yep, I'm used to this sort of thing, and I just say no problem. I'll just show you my e-mail receipt right here as I confidently hand him my phone. Yes, sir, this reservation is for Stella Marie Resorts. What?Let me see. I couldn't believe my eyes. Next thing, sir, would you mind pulling over there to sort this out? I'm like, well, where is this place, Stella Maria? He says, oh, that's on an island, it's about a three-hour drive and a two-hour ferry ride. You have got to be kidding me! Here we go again. No need to figure it out. No need to understand it, Stella Maria, here I come. OK, let's see, it's about 3 o'clock, last ferry at 9, piece of cake. Yeah, if there is one thing in my life experience that's consistent now, it's definitely not a piece of cake.

I know I have to head in this direction and away I went. OK, I'd better put in the port address as I'm coming to some turns. Oh, I'm sorry, you don't get to have GPS, but don't worry; you'll figure it out. That's the sarcastic thought, as my phone, just like the last time I'm going somewhere new, doesn't have a GPS signal. Oh, I'm fully aware that this is just more difficulty and disorientation to break my need for control and the need to know what's coming. Oh my God, did this lesson get pounded into me until it made me sick to think about wanting to know. I didn't learn or let go easily, but I learn well. OK, let's see just how much I can take. An hour later, I pull up onto an intersection, and I instantly know I'm right back where I started, 10 minutes from the Airbnb. I just went in a big circle. If I said this was startling or that it might sour my mood, it would be a lie. Comparatively, this was like me having to drive an extra half a block to find a parking space. Well, I might as well give a proper goodbye to my host. Who knows if I'll ever see her again? And don't you know, it started to dawn on me that this is what the whole detour was about. And of course, me letting go of the need to know. And right on schedule, the GPS starts working on my way out of town. I should have a little time to spare and catch the last ferry. Can't be that easy though. There's only one thing worse than a GPS that doesn't work, and that's one that doesn't know where it's going. I'm telling you, between driving on what seemed just a cow path to a road that hadn't even been built yet, nothing was going to surprise me. I knew I was in good hands, but I also knew there were no shortcuts, and if there was something that I needed to let go, it was going to happen, one way or the other. For some reason, I kept picking the other.

Arriving on the island late in the evening, I set out on what looked to be only a 20-minute drive. The GPS seemed to be working. Not so fast, it likely took me over an hour to get there. I would have been better off using the stars to navigate. All checked in, I wandered out to see if there was any entertainment at this place. It had a very peaceful vibe, and the little bar that was open was very laid back and really lifeless. This was really the first time in weeks that there wasn't a challenge of some sort, whether it be life-altering or soul-crushing. I couldn't sit there for 5 minutes, and I was in my car, wondering what in the world am I doing at a place like this? I hit the nearest village, but that didn't really hit the spot either. It was full of entertainment, but it fell well short of the stimulation I was used to. I imagine this is what it may be like for a serviceman or woman coming back from intense life-threatening war zones.

The next day, with a full head of steam, I headed out with almost a vengeance on this leisurely life situation that I found myself in. There were moments in this day that would have lasting effects. By this day's end, I would thank God for my peaceful relaxing resort I was staying in. Zipping along the windy mountain roads, I was having a blast. Stopping at lookouts and a little beach village, where I met a new friend. All along the way in this Greece adventure, I met the best people. Like a magnet, I found myself connecting with people just beaming with life, and I loved it. After the village, it was back into the mountains and windy roads. It was here that I came to another very difficult lesson. By this point, I knew I was supported in every way, and safety was of no concern. Between my laser-sharp awareness and intuitive response I was prepared for anything. Or was I? My faith had been stretched beyond my perceptual awareness. There were many times visually, my perception would indicate no, don't do it. Little by little, trust came with, if it feels right, it is right. Not once did life surprise me with anything but consistency of my safety. That was going to be pushed way beyond any semblance of my comfort level.

If you have traveled around Greece, you know there are certain drivers that seem to play by different rules. Driving like they're 10 minutes late for their own funeral. Well, I passed one of these drivers, and boy, he didn't like it. Next thing, he is on my bumper, and all of a sudden, something let loose in me, and I think it was the last bit of concern for safety. My hands and feet were slamming through gears, sliding around mountain cliff turns, and passing cars with no visibility whatsoever. There was absolutely no mercy and no possibility this could even happen in any dream or movie set. Even after clearing all traffic and leaving the driver wondering what he just saw, I kept the hammer down, sliding and slamming gears until I found myself standing in front of a monastery. How fitting, just give me my cap and I'll go quietly. It was some time before that driver drove by. He stopped and looked at my car, then over at me, and off he went, figuring whatever that is, I'm out.

As I slowly come back to life, I started to feel the impact. Not sure, but I don't think the car broke the speed limit the rest of the day. I wound down off the other side of the mountain and stopped at a tourist shop when a shirt hanging there caught my eye. It was the color. So I wheel in there and get a closer look. How fitting, the shirt has a picture of a Greek warrior, and it says, No Fear. Like an Incognito awards ceremony, the store owner pours me some of his family wine and we drink to life. He was another Greek who treated me like a beloved friend, and boy did I need it. Arriving back at the resort, was I ever so glad and appreciative of the peaceful and relaxing atmosphere. I'm like, OK, now I get it. It took me the better part of the next two days to recover. And as always when I do, reflective of the difficulty, there is an increase of awareness and higher vibrational energy. Hand in hand, this will also change the people around me and as it turns out, the very place I was staying in. My awareness and intuitive direction is always in alignment with this moment. During this time there was an extreme Fast forward in my process and really my entire experience in Greece. There was and is a certain intensity and change that's happening here in America also. The energy in Greece is simply much higher. Nowhere in the world is energy so vibrant and consistent. So it's no surprise I was hurled into a time warp.

Free Bird

Greece has maintained and protected this divine energy without even trying consciously for the most part. It's in their blood and in the very land that surrounds them, which I was about to discover. Having developed or realized this heightened sensitivity to energy, I wondered why this place carried an extreme calm and peacefulness. Like many of the insights that come, once there is a heartfelt inquiry, it would slowly or suddenly dawn on me. The olive tree, a part of Greece as much as the mountains and sea. Athena's gift is well-received for the culinary benefits. There is an even more sustaining gift that is concealed within. Energy flows everywhere in the world, whether it's high or low. Greece maintains a very high energy. and yet it also preserves the wisdom and vital cultural standards of balance. It's at this beautiful resort that I realize the deeper, sustaining benefit of the olive tree. It's an energy buffer. It cleans and maintains a neutrality in energy. You couldn't fit one more olive tree in this resort. Every path was lined, and everywhere you look, olive trees. Peace in every step fills the air. In the village where I met Penny, there wasn't a single olive tree, and the energy was off the hook. Each individual place carried the energy of the people that inhabited it. Every place I walked into had a very clear, vibrant energy, and not all were positive, and some were very strange. Yet outside the village, the entire island is covered in olive trees, so overall it maintains balance. All nature and vegetation do this to some extent, but none more than the olive tree. So Athena's gift was truly a blessing of divine proportion.

I would often walk the grounds of the resort at night. It was like a different world, magical really. I found myself at the very top, overlooking the valley below. There was this beautiful music softly playing in the background. I sat and felt very inspired. I had nothing to write with or on, so I just composed an e-mail to myself. What stood out to me about this place was, firstly, the peace. Then it was how it never gives you a feeling of how large of a place it is. It has this very inviting, cozy feel to it and I just loved it. This is what I wrote that night. - Small, freedom lives with just cause, complying with each movement, who says where freedom lives in your own heart, life will call you where you are and give you your strength to follow your heart to heights unknown. Together, we open our hearts to see life's greatest season. And together, see a place that calls for love. Eternity sets us free from times long toll, setting our hearts free.

    I've written many poems for people and a few places, and I couldn't recall a single one. I give them without any record. They are very personal, and they're given as a snapshot of their energy and potentially some guidance. The one I shared was a general snapshot of the time and place I was in. Yet it carries a timeless value to it and applies equally now for all humanity. Yes, change is upon us, and though it will have its difficulties, it's for the higher good.

    After writing the poem, I wandered back down the hill and came upon a building with lights on. There was someone behind the desk and we had a little chat. Surprisingly to me, this wasn't all the same resort. The very small lower part where I was staying was not part of the rest and much larger part. He says you should stay up here. Well, although the lower place had a good vibe, this energy here was what inspired me and touched my heart. The next day, it's moving day and there is no talking me out of it. Again, these changes and movements that I do have zero consideration for any difficulty or expense whatsoever. And of course, they give me the best room available. So let's see, I'm now booked at 2 five star resorts and an Airbnb. Oh yeah, once you're booked there's no backsies, and I couldn't care less.

Life gave me 3 experiences that removed all possibility that Penny wasn't my twin. The first happened at the Airbnb, where, in the depths of despair, my heart opened. Originally, I felt like she filled my heart as it opened, but now I know she was already there, and it was just a recognition of that fact. It appears that that wasn't enough because in the middle of this beautiful place, life gave me a 1-2 punch that was impossible to deny. It always amazes me how life creates the perfect scenario to hit me right where it counts. There are only two results that come from these very difficult experiences. I let go of something or two, something becomes painfully clear. And really, they happen together. I swear it requires the most difficult things for me to let go. Remember, expanding awareness doesn't develop the truth; it discovers it. I guess you could say I'm that explorer that took the hard road every time.

Loving my new surroundings, I set out to explore the next day. There is nothing I would rather do than meet new people, and this place was full of lovely, high-energy blessings. After breakfast, Punch #1. Always, do I, have a deep sense of freedom. Yet I'm still subject to the process of an ever-expanding awareness. My awareness is guided in such a way that I will see what I need to see. Hear what I need to hear. And intuitive feelings will create scenarios to bring about insights that bring clarity and also impact. As I stroll back to my room, my thought turns to a gift that was given me at the West Coast resort that I love. It was given with love and friendship that developed there. It was a beautiful notebook with some very kind and inspirational words written in the front. One day since, I opened it and titled it -The Life and Times of Mark and Penny. I thought it very fitting. As I have mentioned before, my experience of time is very different, if at all. Friendships are developed in a very short time, even minutes. Family-type relationships can develop in hours to a couple of days. And they feel like a lifetime of familiarity.

I never see this shit coming and Pow! I suddenly realize the Life and Times of Mark and Penny had already happened. Even now, this thought impacts me. Then, it hit me like a truck, and I was flattened right there and burst into tears. I've been impacted by stronger experience, but never anything with this depth of sadness. It lasted only about 5 minutes before it started to lessen a bit. Directly back to the room, where I just collapsed on the bed and stayed there all day. Oh yeah, this shit is real. I'm far from weak, so it takes quite a wallop to level me. Sudden inspiration gives me a sense to write and I pen a love letter that would melt Athena's heart. I came to know that my insight wasn't a reality reflecting our future, but of the intensity of our connection and the ultimate reality of our oneness. Yes, you would think that would be enough. Two experiences that leveled me right into bed and staggered any thoughts contrary to our being together. Typical, I guess I needed one more, and it pitted my own strength against my own reality. I bet you can guess which one won that battle.

The precision and way that everything comes to me is truly awe-inspiring. There is nothing about me in my depth that isn't known by the divinity that surrounds me, and that's true for you as well. Divine help is kept in check, if you will it, to keep your chains. Or you can open the door for them to show you what binds you and help you unchain yourself. By this point in my process, the door was wide open, and I am completely in the hands of love and exactly where it would have me. The 3rd and final knockout punch would use my attraction to loving, high-energy people to lure me down a road to discover a truth. A truth hidden to perception, yet was revealed to me through trying to let go of the very fabric of my soul.

The next day came with continued effects from the second punch. Though peaceful, my energy would get very unbalanced, and it's uncomfortable. Always, it yields expanded awareness, but there is a cost and it's felt to be unbalance, and disorientation. Very much relatable to an actual punch. One very nice way to help with this is an appointment at the spa. The spas at these high-end resorts in Greece are unlike anywhere I've been. Not to say there aren't other places that could furnish such an experience. For me, the heightened energy in Greece is like nowhere else. And there was no better experience of this than in the spas. The very highest quality of people I seem to meet here. Even more amazing is there was an evolution there that was in perfect time with where I was at and what I needed. Life would suddenly open a door and the masseuse that I loved from previous visits would be unable to accommodate me that day, and I would be given a different masseuse. Earlier on in my process, I learned to not resist any changes because there was always a good reason. Here the elevation started in the resort at the bottom of the hill. After my harsh driving experience, I called on the masseuse on duty at the resort below, and now I found myself knocking on the door at the top, overlooking the valley below. Always younger women, and I was amazed at their maturity and matching wisdom.

Leaving there, I was well satisfied and refortified with balance. Massages were far more than physical; these women are energy healers. They don't advertise this, but it was quite clear to me, and it really helped me. All energy healing really is, is sharing loving intention with another. I do this all the time and it's wonderful, but it's also draining if it's not reciprocated. The energy in the spa is very loving and full of good intention. So, although I received a blessing from these wonderful high-energy masseuses, I returned that energy right back to them, so they also enjoyed the benefit. And the more highly evolved they are, the more vibrant the experience is. I followed it up with the sauna and a shower, and I left feeling like brand new. Finding balance during these times of extremes was well appreciated and is always filled with clarity and amazing experience.

Free Bird

Everyone at these high-end hotels work together as a team, helping the guests to have their best experience possible. They had mentioned a wine tasting the following evening, and I replied, maybe, that sounds like fun. I tried it for the first time at the previous hotel, and I did enjoy it. One obvious thing with expanding awareness is my senses are very keen. Though I wasn't educated in the vocabulary of subtle smells, tastes, and appearances, I was very aware of it. I just couldn't put any names to what I was sensing. Appreciation came about after that, and though I was open to another tasting, I didn't feel pulled to make a reservation and even forgot all about it.

The next evening, I was dressed for anything as I walked a favorite route. Off to my left I see a familiar face waving at me. It was the Sommelier from the tasting I did earlier in the week. (Yes, I had to look that word up) And suddenly, I realized what I was looking at as he walked over to me with a gracious demeanor. The wine tasting, and it was just starting. One thing about these places, yes, they are here to make money, but proper procedure will always trump profit. I was delighted to see him as well and we shook hands and I say, oh yes, this is the wine tasting I heard about. I said I didn't reserve a spot as I forgot about it. He says, would you like me to ask if you can join? I say sure. It never ceases to amaze me how fate has me prepared for anything, and I have no clue what's coming. All I knew was I felt to dress up and walk in that direction, clueless for what or why. He goes and talks to a woman who appears to be in charge. It was a conversation that lasted longer than a formality and he was very appreciative of the OK he was given. Then gave me the OK to come in. It was a beautiful setting, by any standards, and I was directed to a seat next to the only two attending. My friend and previous Sommelier was in an assisting role this time, so I'm thinking, wow, this new guy must be something. I wasn't wrong, and even more was the quality of the other two attendees. Their grace and knowledge of wine was awe-inspiring. Even more though, was the recognition we gained at a deeper level that made the evening even more powerful. It was truly amazing and it's this kind of connection and lovely interaction I came to know, is what life is all about.

There were many amazing meetings like this one, and some were beyond description, and I was about to be blindsided by one. It's time to settle the bill, and the woman that decided it was OK for me to join handled that as well. Our conversation started even before our eyes met and she turned and looked me in the eyes, and Pow!! There was an instant recognition of divine essence. Stronger than any to this point. I was absolutely floored, and I wasn't the only one; she was caught, too. It turns out she was the manager of the resort, and to really amp things up, she knew that I was the one that wrote the poem and gave it to my waitress at the high point dining area. Now here I am, fresh off realizing the depth at which I cared and was connected to Penny, and I'm looking at this Angel in front of me with absolute love in my heart. We talked at some length, as she said, how she appreciated my ability to write like that. There is more that I have come to know in my experiences. When there was a connection similar to this with whoever, male or female, all semblance of priority is lost. It could go on for who knows how long. The stronger the connection, the more lost to the moment. Stumbling over words and her inability to carry on with her duties, I realized I had to say good night. But of course, before I did, I asked if we might get together outside of her work. She comes back with, it's difficult. Boy, that sounds familiar. The concierge at my home resort had a similar response. This woman really had my attention, though. Yeah, I know, that's how it is with all of them. This was different, though. It really hit hard and confused the hell out of me. What is this? Could it be that somehow Penny wasn't the one, and it's this woman? Then I try to squeeze her into the dress, using my imagination, then thinking, well, it might be a little tight, but I think it will work. By no means is she large in any way, but she was a bit bigger than Penny. OK, Yep, she's the one, sorry Penny, we had a moment, but now it's over.

I haven't mentioned, but Evan, my good friend, has been my confidant through this whole thing. So I lay it out to him. Yep, for real this time, Awesome he says, as if he's on board. What now? Well, I wrote a poem for her, of course. It was a good one too. Nope, can't remember it. After seeing how I affected her, I gave her space and just melted into the background. I would see her from time to time, always busy. Once, I spoke with her just a little, and I noticed that she avoided eye contact. I respected it and said good day. While all this was going on, I end up in bed again and I didn't really know why. It was a similar feeling of imbalance and confusion. I'm like really? I was just at the spa 2 days ago. Early the next day, I knew I had to go there again. I surely didn't see it coming, but here comes round 3 and the final punch.

One thing I will say about this entire process. I always had what I needed to persevere and come to a place of peace and understanding. Often I am clueless about the why of things, but I came to trust it, no matter what perception would tell me. Like I stated before, not a single woman I had met in the past eight months took a single step towards me, except the one who jumped into my arms. Coupled with all the writing I did surrounding her and the ridiculous amount of synchronicity, and of course, how everything about us was perfectly matched. How in the world could there be even a sliver of doubt? I have often said I do not learn quickly, but I learn well, and apparently, I require a great deal of pain and suffering to do so. I'm asked at the spa if it's OK if I'm assigned another masseuse. I said sure, that's fine. This is when I really started to take note of how life around me continuously changed to fit my needs at that particular level of energy and awareness. I caught a glimpse of a masseuse there the day before, when I just stopped by to say hi. And I recognized in her a noticeably high level of divinity from the short glance I got from her. Sure enough, that's the one that would be with me. She earned her money that day, and we were both taken by surprise.

The stage was set, walking into the private room, I knew I was in good hands. She had an obvious depth and wisdom about her. What I didn't know was that the massage room for me is a boxing ring and this is round 3. She sets the tone with some background music and scent from some oil. I could tell right away she is very good at her craft. She asks if there is a certain level of pressure I would like or any areas I need worked on. I give her free rein to do as she sees fit, saying I have a high pain tolerance and that I also tend to hold stress or emotions in my lower body, especially my calves. She starts at the top and works her way down, as I'm laying on my stomach first. It all starts out very nice, and I'm totally relaxed. She eventually reaches the calves and oh boy, were they tight. She starts working the knots out, and it's especially painful, but I say no, keep going. Then, out of nowhere, I start to get emotional. I tried to hide it, but she's on to me and asks if I'm OK. Confused, to what is going on, I say no, I'm fine. It's just some emotions coming out, no worries. I'm clueless as to what it's all about, and things start to get worse, and she stops and hands me some tissues. With a look of concern that somehow she has done something wrong. I say no not at all, you are doing wonderfully. I continue to spiral and lose my ability to have any control. She stops again and asks, almost pleads, do you want me to leave the room? Initially, I say no, just continue, it will be OK. I'm just releasing some emotion, and it has nothing to do with you. Hesitantly, she carries on until I realize what in the world is going on. I'm trying to let go of Penny, and the whole thing comes into focus. I say to the masseuse, I think you are right. Maybe give me a few minutes to myself. As soon as she leaves the room, I let loose like a thundercloud, and the rain starts pouring. I found myself in a battle that just kept intensifying. The strength that I've come to is beyond anything I could ever have imagined. And here I am, in a battle for what seemed like the fabric of my very existence in the most comfortable surroundings possible. As always, I fight to the absolute outer edge of my tolerance level, and like a lightning bolt, it hits me. Penny isn't something I can let go, because at my depth, her and I are one. And in that moment, I let go of trying, and everything stopped. All sadness turned to relief and even joy of certainty. The manager left my mind completely, and I lay there in stillness. I was in complete awe of how love or life created the perfect scenario to show me something that was beyond perceptual possibility.

She gently comes back into the room with a look of concern. I say it's all good. It was just a release of emotion and a deep realization. I assure her that it's nothing she did and she finishes without further issue. I leave there with a new light in my depth and ease in my heart. Life would give me one more confirmation. I guess you could say the icing on the cake. Getting back to my room, I text Evan the news. He comes back with a very surprising reply. He alluded to this one other time, but this time he was absolutely insistent. He says you have the world at your feet, and you are limiting yourself to this one woman you met after only being separated from your wife for 8 months. He goes on a bit, but it was surprising, and I generally trust his intuition knowing he only wants the best for me. I came back immediately with, No, you are wrong, Evan. Penny is the one, and you won't change my mind on this. He waited a while and then came back with, I know she is the one, Mark. That was just a brake check to help you know it for yourself. That hit hard, and even now as I write it, tears flow. I did not see that coming! This is so typical of how I'm completely blindsided. This just impacted me far more here as I wrote that than at the time I read his text two months ago. Truly, if you have never been involved with a twin flame, you won't be able to relate to this. It's a slow recognition deep within, like a light flash in the eyes of darkness. This flight is not on the back of a summer breeze. It's more like riding a tornado strapped to a dragon. That was intense, and as usual, after the storm subsides, a still peace surrounds me with a sense of freedom, transcending any description.

Even now, I'm finding a new depth to the gift he gave me that day. He somehow always knew just the right thing at the right time. His heart was guided as mine is, and what a blessing it is, our paths came together for a time. We are no longer in communication as it was time for me to stand on my own strength and direction. Always he lives in my heart though, and continues to give me his wisdom and memory. Evan, if you are reading this in every sense of the word, you are a true friend, and I love you.

Today was a significant shift to balance. I feel even more stable and clear. Today is July 19th, 2025 and certainty is ever present. I see clearly that my time in the States is drawing close to the end. Though the very clear divine communication is still and quiet now, support is ever present. It was conveyed to me in Greece that this will happen, but always know support surrounds me completely. It's actually more all-encompassing than ever before. As my awareness expands into divine energy, synchronicities, timing, and direction become more and more evident. There comes a point where all reference to imagine how it could get any better is let go. Here conceptual description becomes meaningless and won't find its mark. Gone to meaning, knowing fills the air of discovery, left to its own reflection, Light stands revealed, rooted in darkness.

As we approach the end of our time together in this adventure. The feeling it was time to leave Greece became clear. It appears the original planned date to leave is correct and my priorities shifted to goodbye for now. Life wasn't finished with me quite yet, though, and there were still a couple of surprises left. My heart found love and a feeling of home here in this beautiful country, and no place hit the mark so completely as the original place I stayed during my first visit.

Morning came on the 29th of May, and although it was a bit sad to leave another beautiful place with many friends, the memories are timeless. I made an appointment with the spa at what I consider my home base for later that day. I had a close relationship with them and look forward to seeing them. They asked me if it was OK if I had a different masseuse as my normal one was booked. I said yes, that's fine, already in tune with how there is an evolution of my surroundings ever present. Yes, I absolutely loved my normal masseuse, but by this time, I just go with it knowing there's a reason behind it. The GPS now works, except one more little lesson in timing and overcoming what appeared impossible. One turn, my GPS was silent as I sailed by, 20 kilometers later, I realized and turned back. It set me back and had me arriving at the spa nearly half an hour late. My initial thought was to reschedule, and yet I felt no, there is reasoning behind this, so let's see if this is possible. I had just over an hour to the time of the appointment, and the GPS says I will arrive 27 minutes late. The car is surprisingly agile and has decent acceleration, but it is certainly not the Mustang.

Here we go. Little by little, I gained a minute here and a minute there. It didn't really seem like it was going to be possible. 15 minutes out, I caught a break. The road that had been closed was now open and I sailed down the new pavement. I arrived at the gate with one minute to spare. And entered the spa one minute late without notice. They introduced me to my new masseuse, and I knew instantly I was meeting the likes of which I have never known. The divinity that flowed from her was on a whole new level. And as before, she saw something as well. Her presence consumed me from paying much attention to anything else. As I change in the locker room, I barely notice anything. She meets me outside the door and escorts me to the massage room. Already, I'm feeling a connection that I haven't before. She was well in tune and soon had me feeling a connection between us that defied all description. I knew she felt it as well and continued to work her magic. There could never have been a reason for me to want to stop this shared connection, but reality filtered back in, or should I say illusion, and our time was up. The connection continued as she escorted me out. She says, can you stay and help us, out of the blue? I said there is nothing I would want more than to stay here, but I have to go back home for a while, and I hope to return in September. We said goodbye and while I still felt her energy, I grabbed a pen and paper and wrote a poem for her. There have only been two poems I've written for people that contain no instructive wording, and she was one. It was more of a statement of perfection. As I remember the essence, but none of the words.

Back to the Airbnb where I was welcomed with open arms. I said I would be leaving later tonight or early morning. I took a last walk around the village, and I could feel the wind of change blowing. Not just figuratively, but it was unusually windy, and the water was rough. The closer it came for my time to go, the more I felt the pull to leave. The next thing I know, I'm in my car headed to Athens airport without even saying goodbye. I always honor what I feel, and leaving was it. Life had one more pleasant surprise for me as I drove out of town. The GPS was working, but it had me go a completely different way. Going with the flow is now second nature without question. I find myself winding up the side of the mountain. Higher and higher I go, not realizing that this road even existed. My back had been to the village the whole way, and as I turned the corner well above the village, I couldn't believe my eyes. A sunset display that I could never have dreamed of. The whole sky was lit up over the mountains across the Bay. So vibrant and massive, it defied logic. It was a send-off of divine proportion and I absolutely loved it. There are pictures here on my site, Darkhorsepoetry.com, but the real beauty was felt in my heart. I drove away with another wink of recognition and a heart full of love.

Arriving at the airport I was spent and just lounged around till takeoff. Many things crossed my mind returning to the States. None more so than Penny. She got me, and I really don't know what my next move is, but I know somewhere, somehow, we will meet again. Wound up from all the expansion and difficult things I experienced in Greece, it took a while to settle down. The first two weeks were pretty rough, feeling drawn to Penny. Ironically, my appointment to take the first step to my divorce with Katie was on my birthday. Also, ironically, I felt an overwhelming desire to send flowers to Penny. It had been close to a month since last contact, and I knew this sort of thing had to be handled with great care. I called a flower shop I know there and decided on peace lilies. There was significance in the choice that went beyond the obvious meaning of a peace offering. I wrote something short but very clear in hopes of giving her support, but also giving her a sense of space. I knew I would receive no acknowledgement from her, but I did receive something far more telling.

After returning, as things settled down, I started looking into twin flame relationships. Though we reflected many of the normal signs and behaviors, there were a few obvious differences. Her and I had already transcended much of what needed to go. Her heart was wide open and full of love, but still had some lingering personal identification. I was free of identification, but my heart was not open to love of this magnitude. We were each developed where the other lacked, and were hurled into a very aggressive healing situation. We each gave the other exactly what was needed. Neither one of us wanted to hurt the other, yet we said and did things that did just that in order to break open and let go for true alignment. Because of my complete openness to channel, I have the gift of receiving any and all truth that pertains to my purpose. At some level, I knew exactly what was going on and wrote it. Before things really fell apart between us, I wrote to her that we would say and do things that will seem contrary to us coming together. But in the end, we will be together. Yes, I am Privy to these insights, and they are absolute. Having said that, I am not spared from any of it. Not one tear, not one sting of heartache. And I did not have a sense of certainty about our coming together. At least in the beginning. Like any other twin flame relationship, I felt unsure and driven as the chaser. I also thought it strange that I am considered the feminine energy when I'm actually male. As it turns out, 35 to 40% of the feminine energy in a twin flame relationship are actually male in form. We each had come to a place where the only way to move forward was through our meeting. It required something only the other twin could give, and so although our meeting was wonderful and awe-inspiring, it had a deeper purpose that sent us both into the final stage of alignment.

Three days after I sent the peace lilies, my energy completely changed. It went from a heightened sense of needing to reconnect to a sense of calm and attraction to my feeling within. This has continued to strengthen and become my only focus. There were some fluctuations as we are actually taking this journey together. There were two days in particular that were very strange to me because they didn't make sense. After a time, I knew it was something she was dealing with. I just recently had to deal with something very traumatic, and as usual, I didn't see it coming. It was the release of very early childhood trauma. It took a couple of days to filter out, and as always, the expansion reflects the pain, and I am now very clear on my next steps and timeline. This was likely difficult for her too, but I know she also shares my expansion as well. The idea of her and I seems very strange at this point. Really, my whole focus has shifted within, and to speak of her has a hollowness to it. The fact is, the two that met on May 7th are long gone. We each had our things to let go of for balance and alignment. I have come to a real sense of balance and purpose, with no feeling to chase. That tells me alignment is present, which only means awareness of what is already true. Remember, this is a journey of discovery and with it a true appreciation of our infinite beauty. In truth, this is the most beautiful discovery of loving soul essence revealed from the depths of darkness. A divine transcendence from a feeling of separation and unworthiness to the knowing of oneness and worth beyond any measure. Truly, Heaven stands fully supported by the depths of hell, and our shining truth is called into focus through the brilliance of illusion.

This isn't exactly a storybook happy ending, not in the normal sense. Allowing life to flow may be my greatest lesson. So easy it is to want to hold on, not realizing that life here is for appreciation and enjoyment of the truth that lives within all of us. The love that found my heart wasn't for another but the love of my own true heart. What I can say is that in the depths of me, it's more than I can put into words. This is the nature of reality. It has no description; it's just pure experience. Soon, my path leads back to Greece, not to chase Penny, but to enter the next phase of my life. Home is where the heart is, and my heart has felt a pull to Greece since my first visit. When the time is right, Love will open the door, where two flames know only one.

Free Bird

Now we come to the end of our journey together. It's my greatest hope that you have found common ground and a new outlook that will carry you through the changes ahead. Love surrounds you; you need only be open to it. Love will take your hand and deliver you to the freedom of knowing. May your journey be swift and as painless as possible. Just remember, pain is not a punishment, it is a call to freedom and triumph without struggle, is life without meaning. Together, we now find balance, as we step into the golden age of peace, where love rules and kindness leads.

Epilogue

As I wrote this, it was my life relived with the clarity and impact needed for writing the next piece. At first, giving witness to maybe a more extreme sense of unworthiness. Then, gathering wisdom and insights over many years finally gave way to phase two of my process. This was full of change and extremes. It also opened the door a bit more for the reality of divine presence. Then finally phase three, where leisure time was over and real change came in like a tornado and leveled everything.

This is just an example of a process to expand awareness. Every process is different. This is why I will not stress any practice or path, only willingness. That is all that's required on your part. It will be met with a very specific path to bring you to freedom. Moving forward with a willing heart and an open mind will open the door. The energetic changes that are happening in the world will make it increasingly difficult to stay in fear-based energy. It will seem as though the heat got turned up, and challenges will be more regular and extreme. We are all energetically connected, and as more and more open to the truth of love and innocence, the truth will consciously unite in all of us. Yes, you have free will, but as the energy changes, the truth in you will not stay dormant and will remove illusion in its path. This book is meant not as a philosophy, but as a help to those who are open to the changing times.

Free Bird

The changes may feel extreme and unprovoked, but it's just the nature of light shining away the shadow of darkness. Contracted awareness will feel the pain of letting go only because it's unknown how very cruel and limiting it is. Understandably, like a child that holds a knife, who screams when it's taken away. All will be given, and all that is removed is the pain of being something you're not. Love cradles you even now; only awareness may be lacking.

I say to you, O child of God, be still, and I am there. Your heart leads you now. Let there be love and kindness, and the world will reflect your loveliness for all to see. There is no end. Love everlasting is your script. Unseen to you, yet ever present. The Road of Tears has served its purpose well, and now we join together once more in full appreciation of our beauty. Holy are we and Forever One. Momentous is this time of transition, and we shall band together in remembrance with a newfound appreciation so lovely that the prophecy of the Lord's Prayer will finally ring true for all. Thy Kingdom come, Thy will be done, on earth as it is in Heaven.

Amen

An open Heart shall find its reflection in the hands of fate...

www.ingramcontent.com/pod-product-compliance
Lightning Source LLC
Chambersburg PA
CBHW050727010526
44107CB00009B/767